Five Smooth Stones

TO SLAY INTIMIDATION

A Study Guide to *What Kind of Love is This?*

Five Smooth Stones

TO SLAY INTIMIDATION

A Study Guide to *What Kind of Love is This?*

Dr. Susan Marie Pender

Christian International Publishing
Santa Rosa Beach, Florida

Copyright 2018 by Susan Pender. All rights reserved.

This book or parts thereof may not be reproduced in any form stored in a retrieval system or transmitted in any form by any means—electronic, mechanical, photocopy, recording or otherwise—without proper written permission of the publisher, except as provided by United States of America copyright law.

Christian International Publishing
177 Apostles Way
Santa Rosa Beach, Florida 32459
www.cipublishing.org
ISBN: 978-1-7325703-5-1

Published: September 2018
Printed in the United States of America

Scripture quotations marked NIV are from the Holy Bible Thompson Chain-Reference Bible New International Version Copyright 1990 by The B.B. Kirkbride Bible Company, Inc. Indianapolis, Indiana.

For speaking engagements or questions, email
Susan Marie Pender
Susanmariepender@gmail.com
www.lilyofthevalleyhealing.com

Endorsement

The truths from the Bible and life experiences that Susan Pender presents in this book will set you free and bring positive transformation to your life. Jesus said, "You shall know the truth and the truth will make you free." Susan's knowledge and wisdom in using the 5 smooth stones, David used, to portray the 5 Words that reveal what Christians must use to destroy the accusations of the devil and the mindsets that man has caused you to develop, will enable you to overcome.

These truths did not come to Susan just by reading books but by Scripture and life experiences. They have proven true in Susan's life and now she is sharing them with you.

Bless you Susan for taking the time and work it took to make these tremendous truths available in this book. A beneficial read for anyone.

Dr. Bill Hamon
Bishop, Christian International Apostolic Global Network

Author: *The Eternal Church, Prophets & Personal Prophecy, Prophets & the Prophetic Movement, Prophets, Pitfalls, & Principles, Apostles/Prophets & the Coming Moves of God, The Day of the Saints, Who Am I & Why Am I here, Prophetic Scriptures Yet to be Fulfilled (3rd Reformation), 70 Reasons for Speaking in Tongues,* and *How Can These Things Be? God's World War III*

Endorsement

Susan is a graduate of Vision Leadership Institute (VLI). I have had the privilege of training with her and have personally witnessed the remarkable transformation resident within this book. In the current times of advancing the kingdom of God, the Lord is raising up those who will have the courage to defeat the Goliaths that are standing in their way. Five Smooth Stones will lead you through a journey to your own freedom and the freedom of others. It will open your eyes to what is already before you.

Susan's book provides the reader with many strategic scripture verses that put weapons in your hands. One of my favorite things about this book is that it empowers you to succeed right where you are today.

Pastor Joseph Bucciero
Director VLI

Acknowledgments

With a most grateful heart, I want to acknowledge God for loving me and pursuing me, for giving me direction and the grace to carry it out.

I would like to express my gratitude to Christian International School of Theology (CIST) and Vision Leadership Institute (VLI) through Vision Church for co-laboring to raise up leaders with a Biblical foundation and a Prophetic voice to meet the needs of people, organizations, businesses, cities, and nations. Thank you, Bishop Bill Hamon, for pioneering the prophetic movement and establishing this college. Thank you, Pastors Tom and Jane Hamon for your loving hearts, willingness to go into all the world, and for being living example of family.

Thank you, Pastors Joe and Ana Bucciero for these past four years of pouring into me with such love and kindness. Thank you, Prophet Bill and LaRue for the consistent laborious training, insights, and friendship you have offered me.

Thank you, Dr. Tom Hamon for overseeing Christian International School of Theology and making this available for people of all ages, cultures, and backgrounds to study and develop their God-given gifts so they can fulfill their purposes, dreams and desires. Thank you, Dean Susan Slusher for making a way for me and helping me obtain my goals while enrolled in CIST. I am very grateful for all the faculty, leaders, and members of Christian International Ministries and Vision Church.

Thank you, Martha Kontur and Ann Lovett Baird for your patience, skill, and insights in editing this study manual.

Foreword

The spirit of intimidation is real. It wants to affect this generation in insidious ways. It wants to invade and impact every area of our lives. I personally faced its debilitating affects when I was young and found myself painfully shy.

This detrimental spirit of intimidation attacked me when I was young and wanted to diminish my hope of fulfilling the lofty goal I had blossoming in my heart of successfully following in my father's footsteps. It felt like a giant standing in my path and mocking me. You see, my father, Dr. Bill Hamon was a very accomplished minister and a hero in my eyes. Filling his shoes felt like a daunting task that was out of my reach even though my heart yearned for it. This mocking giant standing in my way was trying to break my will and cause me to retreat from my quest. It was then that God placed a powerful smooth stone in my hand to combat this giant of intimidation. This stone was called "the voice of the Lord."

I began to receive word after word from different prophets that my desire was God's desire as well and that He had called me to receive a double portion mantle from my father much like Elisha had received from his spiritual father, Elijah. This weapon of truth from the heart of God was placed in my hand so I could fling it at my enemy and wage a good warfare with the word spoken over my life. Like David, the power of God's word over my life began to shut the mouth of this mocking adversary.

When the enemy prophesies to you about your doom, destruction and inabilities, it's at that time you have to engage in the battle and fight back by declaring what the Lord has said and is still saying just like David did with Goliath.

Don't let this decree of death and downfall stand. When Goliath "prophesied" that he was getting ready to take David's life, David prophesied right back saying 'No! This day I will take your head from you and feed it to the fouls the air!' This powerful use of the word of the Lord will cause your enemy to fall as well.

In this book, Susan Pender does a marvelous job of describing the full arsenal at our disposal to destroy the enemies arrayed against our destinies in Christ. The stone of identity defeats the lies and accusations of Hell attacking our minds, our hearts and personal belief systems. It builds confidence in us that we can overcome and advance past every pain, shame and disappointment from our past. The stone of love causes us to overcome our fears and places our feet on a sure foundation of security and courage needed to defeat our foe and accomplish our mission. It releases God's ability to forgive and live in peace and enjoy God's victories in our lives. The stone of authority is a powerful tool in the hand of the believer that when wielded against the enemy, it hits the very head of this demon of doubt by declaring and demonstrating the power of our headship found in the name of Jesus. The stone of humility is so key because it positions us rightly under the authority of our leader and helps us to acknowledge our need for his help at the same time protecting us from pride and presumption that would only set us up to be the ones that fall. The stone of grace fills us with the strength we need when we feel weak. It releases the very abilities of God in our lives and frees us from the weights of sin and shame and striving so we can advance against our adversary and overcome. When these stones are placed in the sling of faith, they are activated and empowered to slay our enemy. What a powerful arsenal for overcoming!

When we understand the schemes of our enemy and then employ God's strategic weapons against those schemes then we can become the warriors God needs to champion His kingdom cause in our culture in this generation. Like David, we have been given weapons to fight with that will pull down strong men and strong holds and by His victory can change the very tide of our personal histories and even the destinies of nations.

Apostle Tom Hamon
Vision Church @ Christian International

Table of Contents

Introduction 1

The Voice of the Lord 13

    God's Voice Hovers   15

    Adam and Eve Heard God's Voice in the Wind   15

    Noah Heard God's Clear and Articulate Instructions   16

    Abraham Heard Clear Directions from God's Voice   17

    Moses Heard God's Voice in a Burning Bush   18

    Moses Heard God's Voice in Thunder and Lightning   19

    John Heard God's Voice as Mighty Rushing Waters   20

    Elijah Heard God's Voice as a Gentle Whisper   20

    Samuel Heard God Calling His Name   22

    David Heard God's Voice in the Top of the Mulberry Trees   23

    Isaiah Heard God's Voice in a Vision   24

    Ezekiel Heard God's Voice Like Rushing Waters   26

The Voice of Intimidation 31

Identity 53

Authority 67

    Jesus Has Authority   70

    Esther Had Authority   74

Love 91

Grace 107

Humility 125

    Change my Ways   125

    He is the Creator   127

    Price for Humility   128

    The Pursuit of Humility   129

    Consider Others Above Yourself   130

    The Greatest Among You Must Be a Servant of All   132

    Tests Develop Character   136

    The Attitude of Thankfulness   138

    Guard Your Heart   138

Give No Place to Pride	*139*
The Sling of Faith	**145**
Epilogue	**157**
Answers..	**165**
Chapter One - Voice of the Lord	*165*
Chapter Two – The Voice of Intimidation	*169*
Chapter Three – First Smooth Stone – Identity	*173*
Chapter Four – Second Smooth Stone – Authority	*177*
Chapter Five - Third Smooth Stone – Love	*181*
Chapter Six - Fourth Smooth Stone – Grace	*184*
Chapter Seven - Fifth Smooth Stone – Humility	*187*
Chapter Eight - The Sling of Faith	*190*
Endnotes..	**191**
Websites	*196*

Introduction

We all have a book written in Heaven that contains the plans and purposes for our lives. God took time to write these for you and me before our parents even considered having us. These plans and purposes can only be fulfilled after we give our hearts and lives to Jesus Christ and become a Christian. God placed specific gifts and talents within each one of us to enable us to fulfill these plans and purposes for a specific work, but it only becomes accessible when a person becomes a Christian.

Your eyes saw my unformed body; all the days ordained for me were written in your book before one of them came to be.
Psalm 139:16, NIV

All of us have a life course explicitly designed for us as we pursue God and His ways. We were not placed here on earth to live a life without direction.

You have a personal plan and a purpose. God knew what He was doing when he put you in your family, in the exact location, and at the time you arrived. It was to fulfill the destiny written in your book of life.

The life God planned for us, will not automatically be handed to us, but it will require us to make choices to overcome some, if not many, obstacles. This life course will not be walked out without facing and overcoming some opposition.

Many voices in the world attract our attention and distract us from who we were created to be and what we were created to accomplish during our lifetimes. One of the loudest voices of opposition all people will confront at some point is intimidation. The voice of intimidation will hold us back from stepping out to fulfill the purposes we were born for.

This voice comes in many ways such as, fear of man, fear of failure, fear of the unknown, fear of what someone might think or say, fear of not being good enough, fear of not being heard or accepted, fear of not having enough, fear of losing someone we love and the list goes on and on. Every person must overcome these fears to fulfill their creation purpose and experience true freedom and happiness.

For us to walk out the plans and purposes written for our lives, this voice of intimidation must be subdued. If we are afraid to make necessary steps and adjustments in our lives including our career paths, educational opportunities, changing the direction of our business endeavors, living in a different place, or adjusting how we think, we may find ourselves unfulfilled. Intimidation may have paralyzed us.

God created a destiny for each of us and wants to help us walk it out to experience fulfillment. He promises to be with us, strengthen us, and to never leave us. Our lives on earth should be a journey of faith.

We live by faith, not by sight.
2 Corinthians 5:7, NIV

In the summer of 2012, I was living in a beautiful place in the country, had a secure, well-paying job with a good retirement. It was almost everything I had hoped for and worked for. However, I knew deep inside I was missing my purpose in life. I had a deep longing that could not be quenched. Lacking an inner satisfaction, I cried out to God for a long period of time knowing there was something more I needed to pursue in my life.

Knowing that God had these answers, I sought out a prophet for a prophetic word, hoping to receive some insight and direction for where my life needed to go. I had a *knowing* that I needed to change where I was living, and it was causing me much discomfort inside. I had to face the fears that accompanied these changes so I could step into the opportunities before me. God was stirring my heart and I sought insight from prophetic ministry.

The churches in my area did not function in the prophetic very much, if at all. Therefore, I asked God where I could find this prophetic voice in hopes of getting direction. Understanding of the five-fold gifts; pastor, teacher, evangelist, prophet, apostle, I knew that the gifts were designed for equipping the saints and serving people. We can all hear from God for ourselves, but God also set these gifts in offices in His Church to serve and help people mature. I felt an urgency to make some changes and an uneasiness about facing the intimidation preventing me from taking the required steps for change and adjustment. For the first time in my life, I was seeking a prophet for direction. This gift of prophecy is intended to edify, exhort, and comfort.

Five Smooth Stones

But everyone who prophesies speaks to men for their strengthening, encouragement, and comfort.
                                    1 Corinthians 14:3, NKJV

A seasoned prophet does all of this. The prophet will also tell you where you have been in relationship to God, the situation you are in right now, and where it is you need be to fulfill God's plan for your life.

The standard for true versus false prophets is only partially based on their ministry and accurate words. A prophet's words and motive are weighed and determined by the prophet's character and lifestyle. A true prophet will always lead you to Jesus and not away from Him.

After asking God for guidance, I scheduled a time to meet with a prophetic ministry. Our time together was recorded, which is proper protocol when receiving a prophetic word. Upon receiving a recording of this prophetic word, I transcribed what became a ten-page document. While reading it, I weighed it out with significant consideration. Listening and meditating on this word, I had an inner witness of confirmation that everything this prophet spoke to me during our meeting was true. Some of the things this prophet shared with me that day, only God and I knew.

In this word, a spirit of intimidation was addressed several times, revealing how it had negatively affected me all of my life. The Lord encouraged me by saying He would give me five smooth stones, just like He gave to David, to slay the voice of intimidation rising up against me. This prophetic word spoke about obtaining these five smooth stones and putting them to

Introduction

use in my sling of faith. This is a paragraph from the word I received regarding overcoming the voice of intimidation.

"Like David, I told him to run into battle, but I did not send him into battle without arms, without weapons. I gave him five smooth stones. Listen to this my child. I'm going to give you five truths, five principles, five points, that you, like David, will use against the Goliath, the spirit of intimidation that wants to rise in your life. You will never be intimidated again. You will not be shut down; you will rise up. So, like David, I'm going to give you five smooth stones. Put them in the sling of your faith, and send them out to hit the Goliath in the forehead. For a spirit of Goliath has tried to intimidate you for the last time. You will now turn on him. You will now sink that stone in his head, and when he falls to the ground show no mercy, but take off the head of the spirit of Goliath that has intimidated you all these years, says the Lord. Sink that stone in his head, and when he falls to the ground show no mercy but take off the head of the spirit of Goliath that has intimidated you all these years, says the Lord."

Dennis Cramer June 24, 2012

This word is based on the scripture 1 Samuel 17. It describes the setting in which Saul and the entire army of Israel were gathered on a mountain near the Valley of Elah. The Israelites pitched tents for sleeping and made campfires to prepare their food because they were camped there at least forty days. The Philistine army was encamped on another mountain, on the other side of this valley.

Goliath, a Philistine, approached the army of Israel to challenge someone to fight with him. Each morning and evening,

Five Smooth Stones

for forty days Goliath came to test them all. Not one person out of the thousands in the army of Israel stepped up to the challenge; they were all too afraid. Now Israel had fought many other battles. These were all brave and experienced warriors, but not one of them displayed the courage or faith that God Almighty would help them defeat this one large Philistine.

Many of us are like this today. We are fearful to speak up for what is right because someone might not agree with us, or we won't be accepted. We are afraid to voice what God says about moral and ethical standards at places of employment because we will be challenged and possibly lose a promotion or even lose our jobs because of our convictions.

People are fearful to let their voices be heard because it goes against their peers and cultural norms, which do not follow biblical standards. Some are afraid to voice their upright moral opinions for fear that their families and businesses will be targeted financially. Many believers have found themselves in a place of compromise and passivity, neither hot nor cold in their relationship with Christ, which has caused them to avoid any risk at all to stand for truth.

Many people live under this same intimidation today. Just like the entire army of Israel in the days of David and Goliath we have become paralyzed by it. However, young David had something inside of him the other men of this land did not have. This differentiated David from the thousands of mature, experienced and trained men of war. He knew who his God was and who he was in his relationship with God. He knew God would help him overcome the voice of intimidation that challenged all of

Israel that day. God gave David five smooth stones to defeat this enemy of intimidation.

God said He was going to provide me with five smooth stones also. These would be five truths, five principles, five points to use by faith, to overcome the voice of intimidation in my life. As I meditated on this prophetic word, I began to recognize my five smooth stones were hidden throughout the entire content of this prophetic word.

I realized my identity was skewed by my upbringing in an alcoholic family, and in the unhealthy manner in which we related to one another. Disappointments in marriage, strife within my family, ongoing difficulties being a single parent and its negative effect on my children caused my relationship with God to dwindle. These disappointments and difficulties clouded my identity as a wife, mother, parent, sister, daughter, and a marketplace woman. It even clouded my identity as a daughter belonging in God's family.

Identity was the first smooth stone of truth I needed to secure. I would need to embrace the truth of my identity to overcome the voice of intimidation that kept me insecure and prevented me from being the person God designed me to be.

The second stone I uncovered within this prophetic word was *Authority*. Growing up in a home where I saw abusive behavior and later living in an abusive marriage, I became submissive and passive. Because of submitting to this posture, I gave my power away to an ungodly authority, quieting my voice of mutual and independent decision-making. I felt I did not have much power or authority. I forfeited the authority God meant for me to have in my life to make choices, even good choices.

A person without authority to govern themselves feels they have little or no choice in any matter. They feel like they are stuck in a situation and succumb to the hopelessness without an attempt toward a good solution. That is a person without authority, without power to govern themselves. If we do not take control of our own lives, someone else will. We are responsible to guard our heart and utilize the authority God gives to us to rule our own lives.

Above all else, guard your heart, for it is the wellspring of life.
Proverbs 4:23, NIV

God meant for each person to have authority to first govern themselves, then their family, and their territory. This godly authority comes to us from Father God, our Creator as we are in a relationship with Him. A person who knows who they are and their purpose, will possess confidence and boldness. *Authority* was the second smooth stone required for me to slay the voice of intimidation that had been designed to stop me from being all I was meant to be.

A while later reading through this prophetic word for direction in my life, I identified *Love* as the third smooth stone required to silence the voice of intimidation. Without possessing God's love in my heart to a more significant measure, I could not overcome intimidation. Ongoing strife in my family over a period of many years affected my heart attitude toward them and others. Struggling to forgive those close to me, kept me from maintaining an inner peace.

Introduction

No matter how many books I read about forgiveness and tried to apply to my life, I was unable to release the anger and bitterness inside of me. This anger and resentment had to be eliminated from me because it allowed fear to impact my decisions. I did not want to be like this the remainder of my days. The wounds in my heart cried out to be healed. I needed to allow God's love to come back into my heart, even toward those who I felt had hurt me.

But I tell you: Love your enemies and pray for those who persecute you, that you may be sons of your Father in heaven. He causes his sun to rise on the evil and the good and sends rain on the righteous and the unrighteous. If you love those who love you, what reward will you get?
Matthew 5:44-46, NIV

All this contention in my life caused me to lose my first love for my Savior Jesus Christ. All these cares and worries choked this once vibrant love out of me. I needed to forgive others, myself, and God, and return to my relationship with Jesus Christ who loved me first and gave His life for me. The third smooth stone required to slay intimidation would be *Love*.

The fourth smooth stone missing from my life was *Grace*. Realizing that I had become harsh where I used to be kind-hearted toward others, built walls of protection around my heart. In doing so, I became legalistic. The unsanctified responses I had toward others, revealed how my character and personality had changed. I needed to receive God's grace for myself and give this same grace to others. When we become legalistic, we fall from

Five Smooth Stones

grace.

You who are trying to be justified by law have been alienated from Christ; you have fallen away from grace.
Galatians 5:4, NIV

I repented for living according to my desires and ways and asked for God's grace to come back into my life. I needed His grace to slay this voice of intimidation. This would be the fourth smooth stone, *Grace.*

The fifth smooth stone I saw hidden in this prophetic word was *Humility.* It seemed like I was continually going through difficulties; making ends meet financially, strife among family members, setting safe boundaries in court with an ex-spouse caused me to struggle in life. Being a single parent, I was unable to give my children the attention they needed due to my heavy work schedule. Losing my teenage son to a drug overdose, culminated my troubled life. I didn't realize 1 Peter 4 was a relevant scripture for me.

Dear friends, do not be surprised at the painful trial you are suffering as though something strange were happening to you. But rejoice that you participate in the sufferings of Christ, so that you may be overjoyed when his glory is revealed.
1 Peter 4:12, 13, NIV

God does not test us, but He does notice how we handle difficult, painful situations and circumstances. We can allow these difficult times to humble us and learn to be considerate and patient with others as we go through them, or we can become bitter and arrogant and end up with a hardened heart. However, these tests we go through in life are meant to refine our character and cause us to become mature in Christ-like behavior. Tests are meant to allow us to die to our selfish nature and learn to trust in God who created us and loves us.

At the time of these experiences, I did not understand the *wilderness process*. These difficult situations and circumstances bring death to our self-nature and propel us into humility. God wants to cultivate humility in all of us. The fifth smooth stone required to slay intimidation was *Humility*.

In this prophetic word, I recognized how afraid I was to speak up for what I believed was right or to take steps of action. Many times, I was dependent upon other people's approval and lacked the confidence to take the steps that confidence required. I believed other people's opinions about me rather than what God said about me. This lessened my confidence.

When a person is in a situation for an extended period without purpose or joy in their life, they may need to make to changes in their situation. It takes faith to make these changes and come out of the place of confinement. Because of fear, I lived in a position of feeling confined, and unable to express joy and freedom. Fear puts a lid on your personality and who you are made to be.

I also recognized in this prophetic word, I was lacking faith in the things God had said to me. Though He gave me many promises, I was unable to claim them for myself because of a lack of faith. Without faith, I could not take the action steps necessary to move forward in life. All of these smooth stones are

Five Smooth Stones

worthless if they are not put into action by *Faith*.

Faith is the sling that sets these five smooth stones of truth into action. Grasping my sling of *Faith*, I began to set in motion these truths, these principles, to overcome intimidation. Each smooth stone must have *Faith* behind it for it to be propelled into motion.

In the same way, faith by itself if it is not accompanied by action, is dead.
James 2:17, NIV

As David went to the water brook to carefully select his five smooth stones, God provided these truths, these principles, for us in the Bible; *Identity, Authority, Love, Grace,* and *Humility.*

We must research and examine these principles so they become smooth stones, easily activated by our faith. However, before we examine these five smooth stones, let's take a look at what God's voice sounds like in some examples of Him speaking to people in the Bible. Then we will look at what the voice of intimidation sounds like so we can discern between God's voice and the voice of intimidation.

1

The Voice of the Lord

Most people do not realize they can hear the voice of the Lord. Though people attend church all their lives, they may never have the revelation that they can hear God speak to them personally. Although many people believe they know God, they may never considered that God speaks to them and that what He is speaking applies to their lives. Perhaps we have not even taken the time to listen to what His voice sounds like. Throughout history God has been speaking, even before the earth was formed.

And God said, "Let there be light, and there was light.
                                                                     Genesis 1:3,

And God said, "Let there be an expanse between the waters to separate water from water."
                                                                     Genesis 1:6,

In the beginning, before the earth had form, God's voice spoke; creating the earth and the heavens. In the very beginning of the Bible, we learn something about God and His voice; it has a creative power that brings order out of chaos. Chaos has complete disorder and confusion, where nothing makes sense because it has no purposeful function.

When God spoke, the disorder and confusion began to take

Five Smooth Stones

on clarity and form. His voice had a creative force that caused the elements of the universe to shift, separating light from darkness and separating the waters above and the sky below. This is the creative power of God's voice. His voice had to have a clear and direct sound for the elements to obey.

For six more days God continued to speak. The dry land appeared and the seas took shape as the earth responded to God's voice. His voice caused the earth to bring forth grass, and the trees to yield seed after its kind. The voice of the Lord spoke, and the firmament of heaven gave a light for the day and a light for night. Seasons and years came into existence.

The voice of the Lord spoke to the waters, and it brought forth living creatures and fowl to fly above the earth. Everything on earth and in heaven was created by the sound of the voice of the Lord. Then, the breath of God breathed life into man. Man was God's creation made in His own likeness.

So, God created man in his own image, in the image of God He created him; male and female he created them.
Genesis 1:27, NIV

Man was made in the same physical likeness of his Creator God with the same feelings, emotions, and love. If we are made in the same image and likeness of God, then we should be able to communicate with Him by hearing His voice and speaking back to Him.

Jesus was God in the flesh while here on earth. He had ears to hear, eyes to see, and spoke the words He heard the

Father say. This is the same way we hear, and speak because we are made in God's likeness and image. It was the Creator's breath that came into man giving him life. Job refers to the breath of God as the giver of life.

The Spirit of God has made me; the breath of the Almighty gives me life.

Job 33:4, NIV

God's Voice Hovers

The voice of the Lord moves and hovers over the earth and over us personally. It has a force or a wind that moves upon us, upon the earth, and upon the heavens. God's voice creates and brings order to the elements in the sky and earth. If God's voice has the power to do this, surely it can bring order into our lives, and help us when we ask.

Adam and Eve Heard God's Voice in the Wind

In the Garden of Eden, Adam and Eve heard the voice of the Lord God. They talked with Him and He spoke with them. It was natural for Adam and Eve to communicate with God. They expected to hear God talk back to them. They didn't have any doubt whose voice they were hearing because they had a relationship with Him.

When we have a relationship with someone, it is not necessary to see them when they speak because we already know the sound of their voice.

Five Smooth Stones

Then the man and his wife heard the sound of the Lord God as he was walking in the garden in the cool of the day.

Genesis 3:8a, NIV

The sound of God's voice is much more than just noise. Adam and Even heard the verbalization of a particular language such as when people communicate to one another. *Voice* is translated from the Hebrew word *kole* meaning sound. The word *cool* is translated from the Hebrew word *ruach* meaning wind.[1] Adam heard the sound of God's presence in the wind every day.

We have the ability to hear God's presence in our environment also.

Noah Heard God's Clear and Articulate Instructions

Noah was a righteous man, unlike the other people who lived during his days. The earth was full of violence because the people were corrupt in their ways. Noah and his family lived a different life than the other people. Perhaps he talked to God often about all the things happening around him because of the way people were living. God spoke to Noah one day and told him to build an ark. Not only that, He gave Noah specific instructions.

So, make yourself an ark of cypress wood; make rooms in it and coat it with pitch inside and out. This is how you are to build it: the ark is to be 450 feet long, 75 feet wide and 45 feet high. Make a roof for it and finish the ark to within 18 inches of the top. Put a door on the side of the ark and make lower, middle and upper decks.

Genesis 6:14-16, NIV

With instructions on how to build the ark, God continued to inform Noah why he had to build it and precisely what he should put in it. These were clear instructions that God spoke from Heaven to a man, on the earth. God was personal in His conversation and detailed with the instructions. Noah did not doubt that he heard correctly how to build this massive ark. Personal and specific to us as well, God gives instructions on how to create our home, our business, or whatever it is we are building.

Abraham Heard Clear Directions from God's Voice

Abraham heard God's voice tell him to leave his country. God spoke to Abraham to journey to a place that He would eventually show him. God directed Abraham to leave his land without knowing exactly where he was going. He only knew the general direction. Nevertheless, because of the confidence that Abraham had in hearing God's voice, he took action and obeyed.

The Lord had said to Abram, "Leave your country, your people and your father's household and go to the land I will show you.
Genesis 12:1, NIV

Abraham took his wife, all his animals, and belongings on this long journey. Abraham was seventy-five years old when he left an environment that was familiar to him. People who worked for him traveled with him also. He was responsible for the survival of his own family, the families of all those with him, and all of the livestock. In addition, he didn't know where he was going, only the general direction. Nevertheless, he heard God's voice tell him clearly that he was to leave his country to go to another place.

Five Smooth Stones

He had to be confident in the voice he heard in order to agree to the instruction.

Perhaps you are asking God where you should attend school, whether you should take a promotion in another city, whether you should relocate, or how to improve your business. God is able to direct you in what to do, where to go and how to do it. When we set out on a journey due to a heartfelt intuition or an inner witness that we are hearing God's voice, we may not have all the directions and all the answers the first day. It will be a journey of hearing God's voice to lead us too.

We were meant to live our lives by faith in God.

Moses Heard God's Voice in a Burning Bush

Moses encountered the Lord in a fiery bush and heard God speak to him. God used a unique way to get Moses' attention; a burning bush that was not consumed. This visual left a striking imprint of what God would speak to him on Moses' heart. Moses was not able to dismiss the fact that he heard God causing Moses to place a high value on what God asked him to do.

Everything God tells us should be treated with importance, but God will many times use the natural environment around us to speak to us. In this case, it was a burning bush in the desert.

When the Lord saw that he had gone over to look, God called to him from within the bush, "Moses! Moses!" And Moses said, "Here I am."

Exodus 3:4, NIV

The Voice of the Lord

This conversation continues through the middle of chapter four in the book of Exodus. When Moses noticed this bush burning, he could have ignored it because he was tending his sheep. Instead, Moses chose to turn his head and walk over to the bush to take a second look, which led to an extensive and vital conversation with God.

Moses Heard God's Voice in Thunder and Lightning

Moses heard God's voice in the thunder and lightning on Mount Sinai. Hearing thunder and seeing lightning is not unusual, but having a conversation with God at the same time is quite dramatic. Not only that, but there was smoke coming out of the mountain like a furnace. The mountain was trembling violently, and a very loud trumpet blast sounded.

God speaks to people in different ways. Perhaps He spoke to Moses like this so all the people would know by that demonstration God was talking to Moses and leading them. The Father wanted the people to listen to Him and follow Moses' instructions. He loved them and wanted their obedience.

On the morning of the third day, there was thunder and lightning, with a thick cloud over the mountain, and a loud trumpet blast. Everyone in the camp trembled. Then Moses led the people out of the camp to meet with God, and they stood at the foot of the mountain. Mount Sinai was covered with smoke because the Lord descended on it in fire. The smoke billowed up from it like smoke from a furnace, the whole mountain trembled violently, and the sound of the trumpet grew louder and louder. Then Moses spoke, and the voice of God answered him.

Exodus 19:16-19, NIV

Five Smooth Stones

This long conversation continues through chapter twenty. At this time God spoke the Ten Commandments to Moses and wrote them out for him on stone tablets.

I believe God wants to have long discussions with us today also. He does speak to us through the written Word in scripture. If we journal our conversations with God, we may even write down answers to our questions by His inspiration. We should expect to hear God speak to us when things become loud and hectic during our day just like they did in these scriptures for Moses.

John Heard God's Voice as Mighty Rushing Waters

John heard the voice of the Lord as the sound of rushing waters. If you have ever stood by a river that was flowing violently or a waterfall it can be deafening and powerful. The sound of rushing waters can also be melodic and soothing to hear. It is the sound of high energy and force! It causes a person to have respect for the waters that are forcefully moving because they could overcome them quickly if they stepped into it. This was how John described the sound of God's voice he was hearing.

His feet were like bronze glowing in a furnace, and his voice was like the sound of rushing waters.
                                                                    Revelation 1:15, NIV

Elijah Heard God's Voice as a Gentle Whisper

Elijah heard the voice of God on the mountain at Horeb. Elijah had traveled forty days and forty nights until reaching this mountain. There he retreated into a cave and was hiding for fear of his life. Jezebel had threatened to kill him, and he fled as far away as he could until he found a cave to hide in. God wanted to get Elijah's attention and bring peace to him, and draw him out of hiding.

After the earthquake came a fire, but the Lord was not in the fire. And after the fire came a gentle whisper.

1 Kings 19:12, NIV

After a dramatic demonstration of a strong wind, an earthquake, and a fire, a gentle, quiet voice spoke to Elijah. Elijah recognized this whisper as God's voice, and responded by getting up and leaving this hiding place. Most of the time God speaks to us in this manner of a calm, gentle, quiet voice. When Elijah heard God's voice, he was able to get up and leave his place of hiding in a cave.

In a time when Elijah felt confused and fearful for his life, God spoke to him in a peaceful and calm environment that was preceded by a forceful wind, an earthquake, and a fire. Elijah heard the pieces of rock still tumbling down the mountain. He felt the aftershocks still rumbling from the earthquake, and he saw the embers of fire still burning hot. However, when the gentle, calm voice of the Lord came to Elijah, it brought encouragement and direction.

The world around us speaks loudly through our culture, peer pressures, media, and accepted societal expectations. Shouting to us, they pull on our thoughts, emotions, and our will. Contrarily, God is intimate and speaks to every one of us personally, most often in a calm, gentle, quiet voice. When God

Five Smooth Stones

speaks to us, He sometimes asks a question to get our attention through a gentle, calm manner. This is in direct contrast to the sounds of the world.

Samuel Heard God Calling His Name

Samuel heard the voice of God while lying in his bed at night. While Samuel lay asleep, the Lord called out to him. Not knowing it was God, he thought it was his master, Eli. Three times God called out to Samuel by name and each time Samuel mistakenly went to Eli thinking Eli had called him. Wisely, Eli recognized it was God's voice calling to the young boy, and he directed Samuel on how to answer.

So, Eli told Samuel, "Go and lie down, and if he calls you say, 'Speak, Lord, for your servant is listening.'"

1 Samuel 3:9, NIV

Samuel, once again returned to his bed to lie down. A fourth time God called Samuel by name. Finally, Samuel acknowledged God's voice because Eli gave him counsel on who it was calling him. It was God and not Eli. This was the first experience that Samuel had in identifying and recognizing God's voice. When he responded, God proceeded to instruct Samuel concerning his future.

The Lord came and stood there, calling as at the other times, "Samuel! Samuel!" Then Samuel said, "Speak, for your servant is listening."

1 Samuel 3:10, NIV

Today, many people do not realize they can hear God's

voice. God communicated with our spiritual forefathers by means and methods unfamiliar to most Christians. Today people are busy going to jobs, taking care of families, watching their favorite television programs, attending numerous social events, participating in school functions, or doing hobbies they enjoy. God is continually expressing himself to us. However, we are often too busy to hear or recognize His voice among the other noise around us.

The Lord puts His mark on all who believe in Him. We are covered by His blood and have fellowship with Him and with each other. God is a father who talks to His children with words of comfort, edification, and encouragement. God uses men on earth whose hearts are knit with His heart to speak words of encouragement and comfort to others. This is one way God shares His thoughts with us, through someone whose heart is knit with His. Hearing His voice gives us encouragement and comfort. These words will carry compassion filled with emotions to touch our hearts.

> *But everyone who prophesies speaks to men for their strengthening, encouragement, and comfort.*
> 1 Corinthians 14:3, NIV

David Heard God's Voice in the Top of the Mulberry Trees

David heard the Spirit of God moving in the tops of the mulberry trees. God told David, when he heard the sound in the mulberry trees, he was to move quickly to attack the Philistine army. God was going before him in battle. David got a strategy from God and had victory over his enemy. God did this for David many times when he was preparing to go into battle and each

Five Smooth Stones

time God gave David a unique strategy to overtake his enemy.

As soon as you hear the sound of marching in the tops of the balsam trees, move quickly, because that will mean the Lord has gone out in front of you to strike the Philistine army.

2 Samuel 5:24, NIV

God alerts us to the danger that is coming to help us avoid harm. When we are making choices and decisions, God gives instructions so we can know how to navigate through difficulties. These directions and warnings prevent us from harm. He has a strategy for us to succeed in our businesses, to maintain good family relationships, and to be overcomers when challenged.

Isaiah Heard God's Voice in a Vision

Isaiah heard God's voice while having a vision. In this vision, Isaiah beheld the Lord seated on a throne. His attire of garments filled the temple with beauty. There were seraphs each with six wings. Two wings covered their face, two wings covered their feet, and with the other two wings they were flying. The angels were crying out to each other.

And they were calling to one another: "Holy, holy, holy is the Lord Almighty; the whole earth is full of his glory."

Isaiah 6:3, NIV

While still in the vision, Isaiah saw one of the seraphs fly to him. This angel had a hot coal in his hand that he took from the altar with a tong. The seraph touched Isaiah's mouth to remove the guilt because of his sinful condition. Isaiah felt unworthy when he experienced the holiness of God and the temple filled with God's glory. Isaiah understood holiness was surely not in himself. After the coal touched Isaiah's mouth and removed his guilt, God asked this question.

Then I heard the voice of the Lord saying, "Whom shall I send? And who will go for us?" And I said, "Here am I. Send me!"
Isaiah 6:8, NIV

God asked Isaiah if he would go to the nation of Judah with a message for them to turn their hearts toward Him. God asked Isaiah if he was willing to go on God's behalf in hopes to draw this nation back into a relationship with God as their Father.

Isaiah would not have been able to say, "Send me," if he was still carrying the guilt of his own sin.

The vision of the temple enabled Isaiah to realize his guilt and have it removed from him. God brought this question forward to Isaiah knowing Isaiah was in a condition to accept the assignment.

God speaks to us in visions and dreams also. He may speak using a picture in our mind's eye, which may be a vision. God will give us the understanding or interpretation of what it means. It is possible for us to hear God's voice audibly in a vision or dream. A vision is like a dream only it occurs when we are awake. It is like a picture having a thousand words. A dream can also have a relevant meaning for us, but we may need to ask God or someone to interpret our dreams to help us understand them.

Five Smooth Stones

Ezekiel Heard God's Voice Like Rushing Waters

Ezekiel heard the voice of the Lord as majestic rushing waters. This was the only way Ezekiel knew how to describe the sound of the voice of the Lord, "like the roar of rushing waters."

Ezekiel also saw the land radiant with God's glory when he heard the Lord's voice sounding like rushing waters. This was not just water moving quickly down a stream, but it was a roar. This was the only way Ezekiel knew how to identify God's voice.

And I saw the glory of the God of Israel coming from the east. His voice was like the roar of rushing waters, and the land was radiant with his glory.
                                                            Ezekiel 43:2, NIV

God wanted Ezekiel to speak to the people of Israel and tell them to put away their idols that represented worship of other kings. God called it prostitution. He wanted Ezekiel to see His glory coming from the east, through the gate entering into the temple. Hearing God's voice and seeing His glory caused Ezekiel to fall facedown onto the ground. This was frightening for Ezekiel. The sound of God's mighty voice roar through Jerusalem must have been paralyzing for Ezekiel.

God is a prolific communicator and emphasizes His desire to speak and be heard. More than one thousand times in scripture God spoke saying, "Thus says the Lord." [2] The book of Revelation depicts the heavenly realm as a noisy place where a multitude of information is constantly being processed and conveyed to earth. However, most people do not know they can hear God's voice.

God is a Father who communicates with us all of the time in many different ways. When we read the Bible, we can hear his voice speak through Scripture. When we ask God questions and sit quietly waiting for Him to reply, we should expect to hear His voice answer us. This should be a natural form of communication that we have with God, just as a father talks to his children. These conversations bring us comfort and direction. When a voice does not bring comfort or peace, it most likely is not from God, unless He is giving you a correction that agrees with scripture, but even that is comfort.

When we recognize the fatherly voice of God, we can judge the other voices. It is important to recognize what voice is speaking so we can respond wisely to apply these five smooth stones to overcome intimidation. Knowing the voice of intimidation, exposes its origin. Hearing God's voice enables us to guard our hearts and secure peace so we can live out the plans and purposes written for us.

"For I know the plans I have for you," declares the Lord, "plans to prosper you and not to harm you, plans to give you hope and a future."
                                                              Jeremiah 29:11, NIV

After I gave my life to Jesus Christ and received him as my Lord and Savior, I could recognize His voice and how He spoke to me. His voice came mostly as an impression inside of me. It was

Five Smooth Stones

like hearing my own voice only I knew it wasn't mine because the thoughts were not characteristic of my thinking. I began to learn and discern between God talking to me and when it was my own thoughts.

My sheep listen to my voice; I know them, and they follow me.
                                                            John 10:27, NIV

Although, I did come to a period in life when I was not hearing or recognizing God's voice as easily as I had in previous years. At that time, I was not walking as close with God as I once had. Becoming preoccupied with the cares of life, working full-time with an additional second job part-time, and a third seasonal job for more income, my focus in life got out of balance. After a divorce, strife was all around me for many years. During this time, I embarked the path of continuing my college education. Each of us can come up with activities to keep us occupied and over-burdened with cares and stress. However, there are only twenty-four hours in a day and seven days in a week to do all this.

In this single parent season of life, learning to manage time was hard for me. My relationship with God through reading the Bible, talking to Him, and waiting on Him to recognize His voice should have been first priority. Instead, I filled my time with other activities that I thought were necessary. Life responsibilities would have been more manageable had I allowed time to hear God's voice and receive His help.

Our relationship with God is a life-long journey, a life-long commitment. In living here on earth, our lives are much easier when we hear God's voice. Learning to hear His voice speak to us personally, is crucial. Life without recognizing His voice is an empty, difficult, and lonely life.

Spending time with someone acquaints us with the sound of their voice. We recognize their voice even without seeing their face because we have come to know their voice during the time we spend with them. Similarly, if we take time to talk to God, and listen for His response, we will begin to recognize His voice, and how He reveals Himself to us personally. God wants us to be His close friends who want to spend time with Him. God as a Father enjoys talking to His children. He created us for relationship.

God wants to be our Father, provide for us, and to protect us. He gave his only Son as the price for our sins so we could have restored fellowship and a day-to-day relationship with Him. Talking to us continually, God wants us close so we can hear and recognize His voice.

Five Smooth Stones

Questions

1. List some scriptures and examples of God speaking to people in the Bible.

2. What are some purposes for God to speak?

3. How many times in scriptures does God say, "Thus says the Lord."

4. What does God's voice sound like?

5. What are some ways the world speaks to us and keeps us occupied?

6. What happens to people when they hear God's voice?

Thoughts

What various ways have you heard God's voice?

What is the most common way that God speaks to you?

2

The Voice of Intimidation

The definition of intimidation is *to make afraid; to make timid, to daunt; to force or deter with threats or violence.*[3]

The definition of fear is *a feeling of anxiety and agitation that is caused by the presence of danger, evil, or pain, dread, terror, fright, apprehension, a sense of uneasiness or apprehension, concern, to be uneasy, anxious, or doubtful.*[4]

Timidity, fear, or intimidation, depending on what Bible translation, is a spirit and does not come from God. Fear is not a personality and cannot be defeated by positive thinking. Even a person who is an extrovert can be intimidated.

For God did not give us a spirit of timidity, but a spirit of power, of love, and of self-discipline.
2 Timothy 1:7, NIV

Fear is a spirit. Only another spiritual force can break the power of intimidation because it is a spirit. God is a spirit. If we have invited His Son, Jesus Christ, into our heart and lives, then His Spirit is inside of us and abides in us and we can speak to fear to tell it to leave us. That is why we are receiving these five smooth stones from scripture and using faith to activate them.

Five Smooth Stones

We are spirit beings. We are made as a three-part being. We live in a physical body, we have a soul, which is our mind, will, and emotions, and we are a spirit. We were made in God's likeness and in His image. We are a spirit just as He is. This is explained further in Hebrews where it confirms that our soul and spirit are two separate areas of our being.

For the word of God is living and active. Sharper than any double-edged sword, it penetrates even to dividing soul and spirit, joints and marrow; it judges the thoughts and attitudes of the heart.
Hebrews 4:12, NIV

When fear comes, we can sense it and identify it in all three parts of our being. We recognize and feel fear in our soul. We can discern fear with our mind, because of the thoughts it causes us to have. We discern fear with our emotions by the feelings it produces in us. We discern fear with our will because it causes us to respond in a certain way, either to flee from it or take a stand against it. Our will chooses how we respond.

We can discern fear with our physical bodies, because our bodies may become stiff or paralyzed when exposed to fear. When we are fearful, we may experience an increased heart rate, a change in our countenance with worry or shock. Our eyes may become large and fixed in response to fear. It can even paralyze us so we cannot move. Fear can grip our inner man, which is our spirit.

Our spirits will also recognize fear and witness it deep inside. A believer's intuition comes from their spirit inside. This intuition can rightly discern when fear is present and where it comes from.

The lamp of the Lord searches the spirit of a man; it searches out his inmost being.
Proverbs 20:27, NIV

When we receive Jesus Christ as our savior and continue to read the Bible drawing near to God, the light and truth of His word searches our heart motives and beliefs that need to be corrected to line up with the truth of God's Word. Our guilty conscience becomes cleansed and we begin to think differently.

This sanctification process will make us more sensitive to hear God's voice, recognize intimidation, and be more discerning as to what is in our environment. We will be alerted by our senses to a spirit of fear when it comes into our presence. This is called discernment, one of the nine gifts of the Spirit. When we read the Bible and ask the Holy Spirit questions about what we are sensing and feeling, our discernment becomes more in tune with the Spirit of God.

After I realized I needed a Savior and found forgiveness through the blood of Jesus Christ, I began attending a small women's Bible study. In this setting, I began to see the things in my life that were sinful that I hadn't known about prior to salvation and study of the Bible. One such wrong practice occurred when I was a small girl playing with my cousins.

We played with a Ouija board. We asked it questions just like the instructions directed us to do, and it gave us answers. This is an occult practice of seeking information by another

Five Smooth Stones

spiritual force other than God.

Another wrongful forbidden practice is levitation. One of my cousins knew some levitation activations and taught them to me and other relatives my age. We thought it was a game. Even though it seem kind of odd to levitate people we thought it was a game. I always felt it was not a good thing for me to participate in, but no one told me it was wrong, so I went along with my cousins. The adults in my family showed no concern and were even impressed in our creative game playing.

In this Bible study, I found that it was wrong to play with and to experiment with Ouija boards and levitation. By participating in these kinds of practices, I allowed a spirit of fear to enter me and it affected my life. There were possibly other demons associated with fear. Levitation and Ouija boards are witchcraft and occult practices. We give access to demonic influences when we participate in these things.

When you enter the land the Lord, your God, is giving you, do not learn to imitate the detestable ways of the nations there. Let no one be found among you who sacrifices his son or daughter in the fire, who practices divination or sorcery, interprets omens, engages in witchcraft, or casts spells, or who is a medium or spiritist or who consults the dead. Anyone who does these things is detestable to the Lord, and because of these detestable practices, the Lord your God will drive out those nations before you. You must be blameless before the Lord your God.
Deuteronomy 18:9-13, NIV

We should not participate in these things because it gives

access to demonic activity in and around us, which affects our life bringing fear and intimidation.

Do not offer the parts of your body to sin, as instruments of wickedness, but rather offer yourselves to God, as those who have been brought from death to life; and offer the parts of your body to him as instruments of righteousness.
Romans 6:13, NIV

We have gates to our physical body and soul that allows Godly or demonic things access to us. These gates are our eyes, ears, mouth, nose, our hands that touch, our minds that enable thoughts to enter, or any other orifice of our bodies. These orifices are gates that allow positive or negative things into our physical body, soul, and spirit. When we drink poisonous water, we become very sick. It is the same with the things we take in with our eyes, ears, mouth, nose and any orifice including what our hands handle and what our minds think on.

After realizing I needed to repent to the Lord for my involvement in levitation and Ouija boards in order to remove any demonic influence that may have come to me, I was eager to repent. I kneeled next to my couch in the living room. It was quiet, and only the yard light lit up the darkness. I was in an attitude of prayer before the Lord to ask for forgiveness and renounce all witchcraft and occult out of my life.

That evening, I was unable to pray that prayer of repentance because an overwhelming sense of fear surrounded me. A spirit of fear and intimidation was tangibly in the room with me. It was so oppressive that I could not pray. I quickly

Five Smooth Stones

stood up and ran to the safety of my bed.

The next day I called my pastor and his wife to tell them about my experience and asked them to pray with me. I was determined to have the tangible sense of intimidation I had allowed to come into my life, removed. My pastor and his wife invited me to their home so both of them could pray with me. From that day on, I never sensed an overwhelming, paralyzing fear like that again. I repented of all witchcraft and occult involvement, so a spirit of fear could no longer torment me with intimidation at that level again, unless I gave it access.

Intimidation is real. Whether the source of fear is real or imagined, it will defeat us long before we ever go into battle. Intimidation will rob us of joy because we are worried and anxious.

There is no fear in love. But perfect love drives out fear because fear has to do with punishment. The one who fears is not made perfect in love.
1 John 4:18, NIV

The only thing we should fear is God. This is a reverential fear of respect toward God. Fear brings torment and that is not from our Father God. Fear always causes stress and anxiety. When we allow certain things into our lives that are sinful, we open a door for negative spiritual things to enter us.

Let's look at some guidelines God gives us. Then we may be able to identify more areas that fear attempts to overtake us.

The Voice of Intimidation

In 1985, I attended a three-day conference at Hope, Faith, and Love Church in Moorhead, Minnesota. This conference was about identifying sexual and immoral sins in our lives. They offered prayer afterward for freedom from any ill effects of these types of sins. I was aware of some sinful actions in my life whose effects I wanted to be free of.

Previously, the Holy Spirit was dealing with me on these things, and this conference was available. On the last day after the final service, the speaker offered prayer and invited people to come forward.

I would be returning to a home miles away and did not want to miss an opportunity to receive prayer ministry. Sitting in the back, I got out of my seat and walked down the aisle alone. As I got about halfway up the aisle, the minister quickly pointed at me and commanded the spirit of fear to leave me. Now, I was going for prayer about some sexual sins, but this woman minister was commanding a spirit of fear to come out of me.

As quickly as she spoke, my right arm flew up in the air in a twisted fashion without any conscious effort of my own. I quickly went to the altar and knelt in tears of repentance. I knew a demonic spirit had been cast out of me. As I got up to return to my seat every person there was now at the front crowding in for prayer ministry.

A spirit of fear came into me from past sexual sin. Everyone saw it manifest when it was commanded to come out of me. Evil spirits are real. Fear is a demonic evil spirit. However, just because someone is afraid does not mean they have a

Five Smooth Stones

demonic spirit. It may be just an impression of fear.

Fear can be passed down a generational line to us. If we sin in certain areas such as participating in witchcraft, this allows fear in our lives. Once a demonic spirit is cast out, it is essential to keep it out by speaking against it, and not committing the same sin that allowed it to come in the first place.

In the Old Testament, God gave Moses Ten Commandments by which the people should live. But in the New Testament God gave a new commandment which covers all of those in the Old Testament.

Jesus replied: "Love the Lord your God with all our heart, and with all your soul and with all your mind. This is the first and greatest commandment. And the second is like it: love your neighbor as yourself."
Matthew 22:37-39, NIV

We are told to obey all of these guidelines that God gives us, and the only thing we should fear, reverence, and honor is Him. These commandments were given to us by a God who made us and loves us and wants to keep us from living in fear and experiencing intimidation.

The fear of the Lord is the beginning of knowledge, but fools despise wisdom and discipline.
Proverbs 1:7, NIV

One of Noah's sons became cursed with intimidation and humiliation. Ham, the son of Noah, exposed Noah's nakedness after he drank wine made from his vineyard. Because of what Ham did, God cursed him and his descendants beginning with Canaan.

Ham, the father of Canaan, saw his father's nakedness and told his two brothers outside. When Noah awoke from his wine and found out what his youngest son had done to him, he said, "Cursed be Canaan! The lowest of slaves will he be to his brothers.

Genesis 9:22, 24-25, NIV

Canaanite means humiliate and intimidate. This is an "ite" that humiliates and intimidates a person. Humiliation and intimidation work together. Humiliation robs us by causing us to feel weak. The enemy will abuse, victimize, and shame people to make them feel like they do not deserve to be loved or blessed.

Intimidation involves the use of threats or violence to enforce restraint from an action. It immobilizes a person so they cannot press toward the high mark in their life. The purpose of intimidation is to force us into submission by fear. We then become a servant of the intimidator.

Don't you know that when you offer yourselves to someone to obey him as slaves, you are slaves to the one whom you obey— whether you are slaves to sin, which leads to death, or to obedience which leads to righteousness?

Romans 6:16, NIV

When we yield to immoral or unethical practices or things that God names as wicked, we yield ourselves to the spirit

Five Smooth Stones

behind that act. We then become motivated in our thoughts and actions to sound like, look like, and act like the immoral, unethical wickedness that has become a part of us. We, in essence, become a slave to that which we obey. Satan does not have any fair rules. His only motive is to kill, steal, and destroy whatever we allow him to.

The thief comes only to steal and kill and destroy; I have come that they may have life, and have it to the full.
John 10:10, NIV

Intimidation causes us to forfeit our gifts and talents. Instead of using them to the fullest measure in their God-given plans and purposes, we will retreat to where we are comfortable and feel safe. God is looking for risk takers and bold people who are not intimidated and fearful.

We must not agree with fear. Fear is an enemy that must be dispossessed to live a life of freedom and joy. Fear is an enemy and is therefore referred to as an "ite." God tells us to drive the "ites" out of our lives and out of our territories. When we drive intimidation out of our lives, we have a lot to gain. But, we will experience consequences if we do not remove intimidation.

First, let us look at a scripture that tells us what we will gain when we drive out the "ites" from our land.

If you pay attention to these laws and are careful to follow them, then the Lord your God will keep his covenant of love with you, as he swore to your forefathers. He will love you and bless you and increase your numbers. He will bless the fruit of your womb, the

crops of your land--your grain, new wine, and oil--the calves of your herds and the lambs of your flocks in the land that he swore to your forefathers to give you..
Deuteronomy 7:12, 13, NIV

This is what abundant life looks like. No intimidation and no fear! We will be blessed more than any other people. Even the land and crops respond when the people do not allow fear and intimidation in their lives. All of the animals are blessed with health and vitality when man does not allow intimidation. All of creation blossoms with life when it is not under the weight of intimidation. This is how man is supposed to govern and rule.

This is what will be lost in our lives if we do not slay the intimidation in our life. We must acknowledge intimidation as an enemy and remove it from our life and from our territory. An enemy only comes to steal, kill, and destroy. We must drive it out of us and everything we own!

But if you do not drive out the inhabitants of the land, those you allow to remain will become barbs in your eyes and thorns in your sides. They will give you trouble in the land where you live. And then I will do to you what I plan to do to them.
Numbers 33:55, 56, NIV

When someone allows fear in their life, it has a right to be there because the person is permitting it. People are wise to identify every place they have given intimidation access and remove it, shutting the door forever. If it remains, it will be a barb to their eyes. A barbed wire fence is painful to touch. Our lives will be painful and an unbearable way to live if we allow

Five Smooth Stones

intimidation.

Our land, crops, and livestock will also be affected if intimidation is allowed in our lives. This is a high price to pay for not removing all intimidation. Even relationships will suffer, and our relationship with God will be at a distance if we easily become fearful. God does not want this situation for our lives.

God is a loving Father and wants to be in a relationship with us. His hand is always extended out to us. It is up to us if we want to take his hand and walk with Him or not.

If we choose to know God by spending time with Him, reading the Bible, and ask Holy Spirit to help us, then we will receive knowledge and wisdom to overcome intimidation. God is good and wants to be a Father to us. He wants to talk to us, spend time with us and help us overcome intimidation.

God has given us the assignment of governing our lives, families and the territory in which we live. We are the ones who decide what we allow and what we do not allow. The wonderful thing is we can partner with God by having a relationship with Him, and He will help us overcome intimidation and fear in our lives!

The medical field gives us some insights to open doors of vulnerabilities to intimidation. Mark Chironna spoke at the Voice of the Apostles Conference in Mechanics, Pennsylvania in 2013 explaining what causes us to be vulnerable to intimidation and insights to overcome it. Chironna worked as a psychiatric nurse before becoming a minister of the Gospel.

Chironna states, "Psychologists medically determined that the level of mental stability of an average 10th grader in America today, is the same level of an adult during 1950 who was diagnosed as mentally unstable. Another way to state this is, a high school person today suffers five times more stress than an adult diagnosed with an anxiety disorder did in 1950."[5]

He noted, "This was due to the technological devices teens were exposed to over the past two decades. This is the effect that an overload of constant stimuli has on our souls."[6]

If the average sophomore in high school has a level of anxiety five times greater than the level of anxiety of someone in 1950 that was diagnosed with an anxiety disorder as an adult, how much have we learned to numb our feelings just to survive?

Chironna continued, "This continuous stimulus has caused a wearing down of the mind, will, and emotions resulting in instability in the soul. Your soul is what makes you human. The constant influx of information coming into the soul puts a level of stress on us that our grandparents never knew. There is a homelessness of soul and body because of an increase of information. It dehumanizes us. We lose the relationship with family and friends because of this never-ending income of stimuli."[7]

Mark Chironna continued by stating, "We have learned to cope with stress and are in need of having our souls restored. This is a new level of oppression called sensory overload. Sensory overload occurs when one or more of the bodily senses experiences over-stimulation from the environment. Many

Five Smooth Stones

environmental elements impact an individual. Some examples of these elements are urbanization, crowding, noise, media, technology, and explosive growth of information. Sensory overload is commonly associated with sensory processing disorder."[8]

Sensory overload has is also associated with disorders such as fibromyalgia, chronic fatigue syndrome, post-traumatic stress disorder, and autistic spectrum disorders as well. Others include generalized anxiety disorder, schizophrenia, synesthesia, and sensory processing disorder.[9]

Sensory overload must be taken seriously. Fibromyalgia is a neurosensory disorder characterized by widespread muscle pain, joint stiffness, and fatigue. This disease is complicated by mood and anxiety disorders.[10]

Chronic Fatigue Syndrome (CFS) is a condition that causes extreme tiredness. People with CFS have debilitating fatigue that lasts six months or longer. They also have other symptoms such as pain in the joints and muscles, and headaches.[11]

A condition of schizophrenia is marked by severely impaired thinking, emotions, and behaviors. Schizophrenic patients are typically unable to filter sensory stimuli and may have enhanced perceptions of sounds, colors, and other features of their environment. Most schizophrenics, if untreated, gradually withdraw from interactions with other people, and lose their ability to take care of personal needs and grooming.[12]

One wouldn't think that overstimulation of noise and information could be so harmful and wear on a person's mind and emotions. When this occurs, our soul comes into a weakened condition and is readily susceptible to all kinds of fears.

Two different methods prevent sensory overload. One is avoidance, and the other is setting limits. The process of avoidance involves creating a more quiet and orderly environment. This includes keeping noise to a minimum and reducing the sense of clutter. To prevent sensory overload, it is important to rest before big events and focus your attention and energy on one thing at a time. Setting limits involves restricting the amount of time spent on various activities and selecting settings to avoid crowds and noise carefully.[13]

When we experience sensory overload, our souls become weakened and vulnerable to oppression, which allows a weakness and even breakdown to occur in our physical bodies. This weakened state of our soul allows for all kinds of anxiety and fears to enter. This is an open doorway or an entryway for a spirit of intimidation to influence our souls.

Chironna pointed out, "Our grandparents lived in an environment that was more peaceful. There was not all this information coming into their souls. The technological devices we are allowing to come upon our minds causes a download of information for us to process, and we experience little peace in our soul. A soul needs to practice stillness. A quiet soul knows the Lord."[14]

Five Smooth Stones

> *But I have stilled and quieted my soul; like a weaned child with its mother like a weaned child is my soul within me.*
>
> Psalm 131:2, NIV

> *He makes me lie down in green pastures, he leads me beside quiet waters, he restores my soul. He guides me in paths of righteousness for his name's sake. Even though I walk through the valley of the shadow of death, I will fear no evil, for you are with me; your rod and your staff, they comfort me.*
>
> Psalm 23:2-4, NIV

When our soul is restored and quieted, we will be less prone to experiencing fear and being intimidated. Our soul can enjoy peace because it is rested, quieted, not anxious and fearful. A soul that has a constant intake of cell phone information, messages, computer games, television, DVD movies, and noise, cannot be quieted and at peace. The overload of stimulation causes our souls to become weary and then easily subject to whatever is in the environment.

Mark Chironna noted, "If we are watching violent television programs or other media our well-being becomes threatened. We open ourselves up to the vulnerability of receiving a spirit of fear and intimidation. Much of what we view through technology is traumatic to our well-being. Much of what we view has a violent nature. Our environment becomes less peaceful as we allow this to rob us of peace. It causes an imbalance in our well- being."[15]

When we expose ourselves to violent occurrences through media, we are threatened subconsciously. Our threatened well-being makes us more vulnerable to receive a spirit of fear and intimidation into our souls and spirits. It is essential to guard our minds.

And the peace of God which transcends all understanding will guard your hearts and your minds in Christ Jesus.
Philippians 4:7, NIV

We need to have peace in order to guard our hearts and minds. We need to be careful of what we allow our eyes to see, and our ears to hear. We also need to guard how much information and what kind of information is coming into our soul through our eyes and ears to have peace in our heart.

Above all else guard your heart, for it is the wellspring of life.
Proverbs 4:23, NIV

The stimuli we allow to come to us through the gates of our five senses processes through our minds and then becomes written on our hearts. Once information is written on our hearts, it impacts our beliefs that we speak out of our mouths. If what is written upon our hearts is negative then we will speak negative words. If we are speaking negative words, then we hear the same negative information, and it then becomes what we believe. This negativity shapes who we are, and can open us to fear and intimidation. That is why we must guard what we speak because it becomes what is written in our hearts.

Five Smooth Stones

Keep my commands, and you will live; guard my teachings as the apple of your eye. Bind them on your fingers; write them on the tablet of your heart.
Proverbs 7:2, 3, NIV

But the things that come out of the mouth come from the heart, and these make a man 'unclean.
Matthew 15:18, NIV

Unfortunately, with an excess of stimuli coming into our souls, guarding our hearts and what gets imprinted upon them is more difficult to protect from harm. We are the only ones who can guard our hearts. No one else can do this for us. God is the God of peace. Peace originated with God. Where peace is, there can be no fear or intimidation. For us to have the same peace that God has, we need to spend time with Him and time in the Word. We have to get this peace from Him and then guard it.

Now may the Lord of peace himself give you peace at all times and in every way. The Lord be with all of you.
2 Thessalonians 3:16, NIV

There is not anything wrong in watching the news and keeping up with world events, but to be consumed with it and have a steady diet of it without the balance of positive, uplifting information, may cause one to look at their future with a pessimistic attitude and fear. If we are taking in a constant flow of information and do not allow time to enjoy the rest that nature brings to us, and the joy of uplifting, positive fellowship with people around us, it can cause a weariness to settle on our souls. Weariness is physical or mental exhaustion by hard work,

The Voice of Intimidation

exertion, and strain, characterized by fatigue.[16]

Come to me, all you who are weary and burdened, and I will give you rest. Take my yoke upon you and learn from me, for I am gentle and humble in heart, and you will find rest for your souls.
                                                                Matthew 11:28-29, NIV

I will refresh the weary and satisfy the faint.
                                                                Jeremiah 31:25, NIV

Our hearts easily become unguarded at this place of weariness, and peace will leave us. This makes us vulnerable to fear for our safety and security. In Nehemiah 4 we can see an example of this when the Jews were rebuilding the walls of their city.

When Sanballat heard about this, he sent his army to stop them. Sanballat was an enemy of the Israelite people and made several attempts to halt Nehemiah from rebuilding the walls of Jerusalem. The people had a sword in one hand and built with the other hand. They continued night and day building their walls and keeping the enemy away. Sanballat was attempting to put fear in the Jewish people so they would stop the building process. The enemy came against their minds in an attempt to cause them to grow weary and to go insane.

They were in constant battle with the sword in one hand fighting for their lives and trying to rebuild the walls of their city with the other hand. The enemy invariably fought against them to weary their minds.

Five Smooth Stones

However, as the people worked together, supporting each other, helping each other complete the task, they eventually completed the walls of their city. In this way, they overcame the tactic of fear to overtake them.

We can overcome fear by helping each other and by praying for one another, thereby carrying each other's burden. This help and support of love and prayer provides an environment of peace and rest in a community.

Barbara Yoder states in her CD teaching *Overcoming the Goliath of Fear*, "The story of Nehemiah, demonstrates a wearing down of the mind and emotions along with the physical overload. This causes instability and weakens the will of a person until they want to give up on whatever is important to them. The result of fear is insanity because it drives people to an absence of sound judgment. Nehemiah prevented this by encouraging the people to work together, in an organized fashion, and loving each other. This became their foundation for their survival and overcoming intimidation."[17]

Yoder continues, "When people do not love each other and do not invest in relationships to foster unity, they become vulnerable to perversion in their relationships, have unhealthy relationships, and indulge in more alcohol and drug use. These are all wide-open places for fear and intimidation to enter. This fear leads to irresponsible financial decisions, sickness, and infirmity."[18]

God wants us to be strong and stand on a firm foundation as Nehemiah did. Foundations will be tested just like in the days of Nehemiah. We must be aware of the vulnerabilities that cause us to be susceptible to fear and intimidation.

By recognizing the voice of intimidation, we can identify fear. When we know what our enemy sounds like and looks like, we can identify it and then strategize how to overcome it. Intimidation and fear need to be overcome in our lives to fulfill our purposes which God wrote in our books before we were born. God gave us these truths and principles to slay intimidation, just like he gave David five smooth stones to slay Goliath.

Gathering our five smooth stones, we will become skilled in using what God puts in our hands and overcome the voice of intimidation. The first smooth stone we will take into our possession is *Identity*.

We will examine *Identity*, and how to obtain it, and then activate it in our lives so we can slay intimidation and fear.

Questions

1. What is the meaning of Canaanite?

2. What are the consequences if we do not remove intimidation from our lives?

3. What will we gain if we do remove intimidation from our lives?

4. In what three parts of our person do we sense fear and can identify it?

5. List some guidelines God gives us for living.

6. What two ways do we quiet the sensory overload the world environment sends to our body, soul, and spirit?

7. Describe some disorders associated with sensory overload.

8. What things cause our souls to become weary and easily subject to whatever is in the environment?

3

Identity

Let's walk together along the water brook of God's word and uncover the first smooth stone of *Identity*. We need to be grounded and secure in the truth of who we are so that the voice of intimidation cannot cause us to fear who God says we are.

The definition of Identity is *the condition or fact of being the same or exactly alike, sameness; oneness. The condition or fact of being a specific person or thing; individuality. The characteristics and qualities of a person considered collectively and regarded as essential to that person's self-awareness. The condition of being the same as a person or thing described or claimed.*[19]

Identity is the condition or fact of being the same or having the likeness of another. God created us to have His same likeness.

So, God created man in his own image, in the image of God, created he him, male and female created he them.
Genesis 1:27, NIV

Male and female are both made in the likeness of God. We are meant to have the same likeness and image that God has while we are living on earth. We were made in His image. His image has three parts; a spirit, a soul, and a body. The Bible explains that we are triune beings. We are a spirit, with a soul,

Five Smooth Stones

which is our mind, our will, and our emotions, and we live in a body. This is how God made us and how we function on the earth.

God is Spirit.
                                              John 4:24a, NIV

First, we are spirit beings, just as God is a spirit. Second, we have a soul consisting of a mind to think. Our will to make choices and decisions for ourselves is in our soul. Ours soul also contains emotions that has feelings about our environment and for one another. Third, God gave us physical bodies to inhabit while we are here on earth. This is our outward physical appearance and it provides us a means to function in the earth. God told us to be fruitful and multiply and meant for us to love Him and to love one another.

Jesus was a generated Son, a seed from the loins of God. Jesus' lineage began with Abraham and came all the way down to Mary. Jesus was the direct seed of God, therefore the firstborn in the lineage of those who are spiritually born of God. God is literally the Father of our Lord Jesus Christ. Jesus is in all reality the only begotten Son of the eternal God. The Eternal God fathered the physical body of Jesus, which was crucified, buried, resurrected, and re-inhabited by Jesus. He was immortalized and eternalized. Jesus' flesh and bone body is the only human body in the triune Godhead.

For in Christ all the fullness of the Deity lives in bodily form.
                                              Colossians 2:9, NIV

Identity

The human race was patterned after His blueprint, the body of Jesus. God planned from eternity to have a Son with a body, soul, and spirit, in an earthen body as well as a spiritual body. The birth, life, death, and resurrection of Jesus were all planned before Adam was created and placed on planet earth. From man's perspective, Jesus came into existence as a mortal being because of mankind's need for redemption.

Through the creation of man, God fulfilled three desires: His desire for a family, His desire for His Son to take on a human body and be our God forever, and His desire to fashion human bodily temples as a dwelling place for His Spirit.[20] Therefore our identities first come from God. He is our Creator. He is our Father. We were meant to look, act, and function just like He does.

The next influential source of identity comes from our parents. God blessed a marriage between man and woman and purposed them to be fruitful and to multiply in the earth by having children. The home was meant to have a father and a mother who were to be loving parents providing a safe and secure environment for their family. The original intent for the family was to display an earthly example of what family looks like in heaven. Our identity comes from God and then should be reinforced and nurtured within our family here on earth.

Our parents were purposed to reinforce our identities by loving and properly training us to love God and our neighbors. God sets the father in the home as the provider and the protector, which is a reflection of God, our Father in Heaven. God is the original provider and protector of man. The father

Five Smooth Stones

provides family members with a warm and safe home to live in, enough food to eat, and clothes to wear. He encourages his children to fulfill their dreams, by advising them on endeavors or career paths that may fulfill them, even offering financial support to attend college or start a business. Fathers were meant to be examples of how to live happily, prosper and love and nurture their children.

Fathers are granted this position as head of the home by God. They are purposed to provide safety and security for the family. The father was intended to convey to their children this fatherly identity of love, value, and a secure sense of who they are created to be so they can fulfill their call and destiny.[21]

The vital position of the father in the home was preordained to be a blessing to the family. God's intention was to transfer His identity to the father, who would, in turn, convey these attributes into the lives of their children. The children receive this impartation of identity while growing up in the home·

For the husband is the head of the wife as Christ is the head of the church, his body, of which he is the Savior.
Ephesians 5:23, NIV

Children, obey your parents in the Lord, for this is right. Honor your father and mother which is the first commandment with a promise.
Ephesians 6:1, 2, NIV

Fathers impart identity to their children. A mother imparts much into a child also, but God has appointed the father as the leader and overseer of the family. When a father does not fulfill the role God gave him, the children will not have the imprint of their God-given identity upon their heart. They will be left to search out their identity in order to know who they really are. We all have a natural desire to know who we are and why we are here. If a person does not have their identity imparted to them by their father, they will naturally embark on a search to fill that void. Identity and destiny are wrapped up together.[22]

When we achieve our value through what we do and accomplish, we will not have a true understanding of who we are.

If the father misuses his position over the family, causing them to feel threatened or uncared for, it will distort the true identity of the child which was supposed to have been imparted to them. When children grow up in abusive homes, they may not have a true identity of themselves.[23]

Without a strong identity of who they are, there remains a vulnerability to intimidation and fear. They may carry negative emotions in their character and personality if their identity is not imparted the way God intended it to be while in their home. Some of these negative emotions in their character and personality may be insecurity and many kinds of fear. This is not the identity God meant for us to have. Without knowing the truth of who we are created to be we will not have the confidence inside of us to face intimidation.

This lack of identity stems from a society where too often fathers have abandoned their children and single mothers have carried the load alone. Statistics reveal that one in four kids under the age of eighteen will be raised without a father involved in their lives. Even if the father is physically present in the home, he may be emotionally absent or uninvolved.

For years, men have been devalued and emasculated by television programs and movies that portray them as foolish and lacking strength. It should not be surprising that we have such a crisis of identity and gender in our nation today. This is a spiritual crisis, a heart issue that has manifested in the physical realm.[24]

I was one who carried this insecurity and fear into my adult life. I was well cared for physically in my home and always had enough nutritious food, clothes, a warm home and so many exciting activities living on a farm, but because of my father's behavior when consuming alcohol there was a lack of emotional stability and security in our home. Not until I was twenty-three years old and deeply searching for who I was and the meaning of my life, did I find forgiveness for my own sins, and begin to claim my true identity in Christ and the purposes God had for my life.

After inviting Christ into my heart, I began to overcome the insecurity and fears lodged in my soul that covered my true identity. The Holy Spirit was faithful to show me the things from which I needed to be free. Little by little He peeled sin's effects off me. Intimidation and fear were often connected to each layer of sin. Sometimes, before our identity can come forth, we have to remove ourselves from certain environments, even the places we live in order to remove the lid that is placed on our identity.

Melodye Hilton states in her book Higher Living Leadership, "Our identity also comes from our formal teaching and our culture. These are known as adapted values. These can become lids over us that do not allow us to release who we are beyond the environment and culture we live in. Positioning ourselves in an environment that gives us an opportunity to grow according to the desires within us, can remove the lids of past expectations placed on us so that our identity can more fully develop."[25]

Dr. Hilton also notes, "Our innate values come from God. They are God's dream for us, our DNA, our identity, and our contribution to the world. Having an awareness of *our place in history* will solidify our convictions and propel us forward. When we look to our Creator God and let Him imprint our identity upon our heart, then we can fully comprehend who we are in our family, in our community, and in our world."[26]

Our identity is intended to include a sense of right and wrong along with the ability to speak up for ourselves and make good choices. This is a Godly-impartation that was meant to come from our parents, especially the father. We were created by God to have dominion and rule over our own lives and over creation. We were meant to discover our talents and gifts within the protection and safe environment of our home.

Identity is given to each person as a blessing. Our identity and character should reflect God's identity because we were made in the image of God, Himself. Abuses and lies rob us of who we were created to be, and the purposes within us.

If you don't know your identity you are susceptible to being what others want you to be or whatever the environment may reflect on you. If you show weakness in your character, you may easily succumb to anyone or anything that overpowers you.

God wants us to be strong and remain on His firm foundation of His Word. When we do not have this firm foundation to build our house on, it will sway with any wind that comes along. We will give the control of our lives over to other people and other ideas that may not be healthy for us.

A person may attach to a substance, or chemical, alcohol, eating disorder or sexual promiscuity because of an emptiness inside of them due to the lack of validation. This addiction will then define who they are and it will become their identity.[27]

A person's sexuality is also at the very core of their identity. When parents demonstrate genuine love to their children, they impart the child's identity to them. When love is demonstrated by those in authority in the home, sexual identity is reinforced. This is where a person is firmly grounded in their womanhood or manhood.

Family was God's plan for protection and nourishment by the father and mother so they can impart gender validation to their children. In contrast, if the parents do not impart love, acceptance, and intimacy to the child in a godly manner it will create a void within the child. This void will be filled by something else, which will be a perversion of what is right, good, and true. It may disclose as incest, pornography, fornication, various addictions, codependency, rejection, insecurity and fear.[28]

Identity

When children do not get to participate in the process of decision making in the family, it hinders their own decision-making ability. If they are not properly instructed in discerning right from wrong, and how to respond appropriately to people, they will lack proper discernment. Consequently, if a parent does not teach children to discern which people are safe and which ones are not safe, they will not act with sound judgment. This causes a fracture in their identity because they cannot discern the environment around them allowing fear and intimidation to invade their personality and causing them to be nervous or overly anxious.

Without sound discernment, a person will not be grounded in who they are because they are not seeing themselves rightly. Decisions are made based on what a person believes about themselves in relationship to their environment.

No one else can fulfill another person's potential. Each person has to embark on their own quest to discover why they are on this planet, what makes them get out of bed in the morning, and what they uniquely contribute to the world. This derives from how they view themselves. Many people never obtain a vision for their life because they do not know who they are as an individual. They stumble blindly and aimlessly throughout life existing only at a level of survival. Others may receive insight and vision of their purpose, but lose sight of it because of traumatic events, or through their own neglect.

Where there is no revelation, the people cast off restraint; but blessed is he who keeps the law.
Proverbs 29:18, NIV

Five Smooth Stones

With no vision, there is no hope or direction. When we do not have a clear understanding of our identity and who God made us to be we will not know our calling or how to live that out.

Discovering your identity so you can achieve a worthwhile purpose has a cost of pain to be endured. Only vision can give purpose to the pain endured while walking it out to reach your goal. The good news is pain and difficult circumstances do not define you. Only God's Word gives a definition of your identity and your purpose for being. Christ demonstrated this incredible power of vision to enable you to endure and progress with your eyes on your goals. God is the author and finisher of who you are and of your purpose.

Let us fix our eyes on Jesus, the author, and perfector of our faith, who for the joy set before him endured the cross, scorning its shame, and sat down at the right hand of the throne of God.
Hebrews 12:2, NIV

We were all created by God, having all come from the first man and woman, Adam and Eve. Because sin entered the world, we became separated from God. In the Old Testament, the blood of lamb sacrifices were given to cleanse the people of sin. When Jesus came into the world and died on the cross, He paid man's debt for sin in full. Man is required to believe in and accept the price Jesus paid.

This is how we become children of God and receive eternal life. This is how we become reconciled back to God. This is how a person receives the identity they were meant to have.

Identity

To secure the first smooth stone of *Identity* we must receive Jesus Christ as our savior and abide with Him by reading the Bible and communicating with Him daily. There must be repentance for one's sin, and an acknowledgment of a need for a redeemer. With a desire to have these sins, and our sin nature washed away by the blood of Jesus, we need Jesus Christ to be our Lord and Savior.

That if you confess with your mouth, "Jesus is Lord," and believe in your heart that God raised him from the dead, you will be saved. For it is with your heart that you believe and are justified, and it is with your mouth that you confess and are saved.
Romans 10:9-10, NIV

Accepting Jesus Christ as your Savior and Lord of your life places you within the family of God. When you receive Him, you have a new identity. You are a child of God and belong to God's family. Your identity is in Christ Jesus.

Therefore, if anyone is in Christ, he is a new creation: the old has gone, the new has come!
2 Corinthians 5:17, NIV

The Bible is God's inspired Word. It is God's Word breathed into man by reading, understanding, and accepting it as the compass that directs you. By reading it and talking to God, you will gain wisdom and understanding that will help you walk out your lives each day. God will talk to you every day. He will always be with you because He wants to have a life-long relationship with you.

Five Smooth Stones

Take up the Smooth Stone of Identity
I take up this smooth stone of Identity and receive Jesus Christ as my Savior and as the Lord of my life. I realize I am lost in this world and I see my need for a Savior. Thank You, Jesus for paying my debt of sin with Your own blood on the cross. Father, thank you for imparting my Identity into me by imparting Your Spirit into me through Jesus Christ. Now, I ask You Lord to teach me Your will and Your ways.

The second smooth stone that is required to slay the voice of intimidation is called *Authority*.

Being in the family of God has many wonderful benefits and blessings. One of them is authority. We will uncover this truth along the river, from under the clay, and polish it, bringing it into our possession to its rightful place. Intimidation will not have any negative interference in fulfilling the plans and purposes written in our books in heaven.

Let's begin our discovery of *Authority*.

Questions

1. What is identity?

2. What does it mean that we have the same likeness of God?

3. Describe the three parts that make up a human being.

4. After God who should be the most influential that imparts identity to us?

5. What things might hinder our identity being imparted into us?

Thoughts

Are there places of your identity that are lacking compared to how Father God sees you? What are they?

Five Smooth Stones

4

Authority

Let's continue by securing our second smooth stone; Authority.

The definition of authority is *the power or right to give commands, enforce obedience, take action, or make final decisions, the position of one having such power. Such power as delegated to another, authorization, warrant. The power or influence resulting from knowledge, prestige. The citation of a writing, decision, etc. in support of an opinion, action.*[29]

Authority is delegated power. Policemen who direct traffic during the rush hour only need to raise their hands and the cars will stop. These men don't have the physical ability to stop the vehicles if the drivers choose not to stop. They don't use their own strength to stop traffic. They are strong in the authority that is invested in them by the government they serve. People recognize this authority and will, obey by stopping.

Policemen are given this authority by the government that supports them to serve the people and provide safety. They have written regulations and policies so they can follow established rules and laws. This is how they know where their boundaries are and how they are required to function within the sphere of authority they have been given. The main purpose of policemen is to restrain evil, protect innocent people, and provide a safe environment in which to live.

Officers in the military branches of the army, navy, marines, and coastguard are given authority over the people they train and lead. This is also for the purpose of service and safety. Their authority comes from the government that backs them.

The military have written regulations and policies that they follow. These rules and laws provide guidelines and boundaries within which their authority functions. The military's purpose is to restrain evil and protect people in a territory providing them with safety so they can live in peace.

People who are in upper management of a business have delegated authority to train and lead that organization so that it prospers. Policy and Procedure Manuals contain written guidelines for training the people and running the business. Leaders are not only given authority to direct and serve the people employed by their organization, but to serve the customers who use their products to improve their lives. These leaders who have authority to serve employees or customers have a responsibility to make wise decisions so their organization prospers and fulfills its purpose. This gives the people within the organization safety and security while meeting the needs of customers.

As police, military officers, and managers have authority within their spheres of influence, so it is in the Kingdom of God. Authority was delegated to man at creation.

Then God said, "Let us make man in our image, in our likeness, and let them rule over the fish of the sea and the birds of the air, over the livestock, over all the earth, and over all the creatures that move along the ground."

Genesis 1:26, NIV

Authority is a legal state, a legal position. Man was given authority on the earth to rule over all God created, and to care for all that God placed on the earth. It is a delegated power God gave to man to care for one another, our families, and the area we live in. We are to rule and govern our own lives, our families, and the territory we live in. God commanded us to take up this authority that he gives to us and rule just like He would to protect and care for everything in the earth.

God has provided the Bible as a manual for our lives. It contains the rules, policies, and guidelines for life. God gives us authority when we are born again. We do not need to understand the contents of the entire Bible, but we will need to read and study the Bible to begin to understand the will and purposes of God so we know how to administer the authority God has given to us. As we read and study the Bible and walk in relationship with God this becomes our training period. Police, military officers, and business leaders all require a training period and a maturity level before given the responsibility to administrate their authority to serve and protect. God's intends that we rule with authority over ourselves, our families, and our territories.

First, we learn to govern ourselves rightly. When we

Five Smooth Stones

become mature at that level, we can govern our own families. Our depth of relationship and submission to God determines how we govern ourselves and our families. If we have a relationship to the One who has all authority in Heaven and in the earth, and we have knowledge and understanding of His manual, including how to operate on the earth, then we have access to much authority. The size of the territory we govern, whether it is business, land, or people, will be determined by our submission to and by our relationship to the One who backs up our authority; God.

We enforce this authority much like the secular authorities in our communities do. It is for the purpose of restraining evil and maintaining a safe environment with the intent of allowing people to prosper in all areas of life. There are ways of restricting and even punishing those who threaten our safe environment depending on the degree of violation that was inflicted. Throughout the scriptures, there are historical examples of God's authority exercised in people's lives.

Jesus Has Authority

God gave Jesus authority over all demons. It was delegated authority that originated with God the Father. Authority is delegated power given to another to function in the same authority and on behalf of the one who is the source of that power. Jesus did not have authority in himself, but it was given to him by the One who had all authority and all power, God the Father, Creator of heaven and earth.

Authority

> *Then Jesus came to them and said, 'All authority in heaven and on earth has been given to me.*
>
> Matthew 28:18, NIV

Jesus Christ, who is now at the right hand of the Father in heaven, gave this same authority to those who believe in Him, and have received him as the one who died for their sins. Believers have been assigned this same authority on the earth to rule over demons. This is a lot of authority!

> *I have given you authority to trample on snakes and scorpions, and to overcome all the power of the enemy; nothing will harm you.*
>
> Luke 10:19, NIV

When we are made new creatures in Christ Jesus, we inherit the name of the Lord Jesus Christ, and we can use His name in prayer against the enemy, satan, and demonic spirits.

When you are born again by receiving Jesus Christ as your Savior, your spirit is quickened and comes alive. Just like you are born in the natural and come to life, when you receive Jesus Christ as your Savior your spirit man comes alive. You then have the same spirit of Christ inside of you that Jesus had when he lived on the earth. This all comes from God, the Father, as your inheritance in the earth.

God himself is the power behind our authority. The devil and his forces are obliged to recognize His power. The believer who thoroughly understands that the mandate of God is backing him, can exercise his authority and confidently face the enemy.

Five Smooth Stones

We should not be fazed by any voice of fear that attempts to challenge the voice of the Lord inside of us. When we belong in the family of God, everything He has, becomes ours. It is part of our rightful inheritance to receive the same authority that our father has.

Our natural family name represents something in the earth. It may be who we are, what kind of business we are involved in, or what kind of reputation we have. Each generation will inherit what that family name represents whether it is good or bad. We receive that inheritance from our family because of the name we are given. If we inherit a bad reputation or a negative representation from our family name, God can redeem that and cause us to begin a generational blessing of a good inheritance.

It is the same in God's family. We have an inheritance which includes authority. We can use this authority over demonic powers because the Spirit of God within us is greater than the spirit that is in the world with satan. This authority is vested in us by the Lord Jesus Christ; therefore, we are strong in who we are in the Lord.

You dear children, are from God and have overcome them because the one who is in you is greater than the one who is in the world.
                                                                1 John 4:4, NIV

Finally, be strong in the Lord and in his mighty power.
                                                                Ephesians 6:10, NIV

When confronting intimidation, we can raise our hand and

command fear to not come any closer. It must obey our voice because it is backed by the voice of God. The policeman knows his position and stops vehicles with the simple raising of his hand. This is the immense power God has bestowed upon His children who believe what He says. When we know who our father is and what belongs to Him also belongs to us, then we know without a doubt that we have that same authority our father has.

When Jesus had called the twelve together, he gave them power and authority to drive out all demons and to cure all diseases.
Luke 9:1, NIV

Originally, God made the earth and the fullness of it, giving Adam dominion over all the works of his hands. Adam committed high treason by sinning against God, and therefore he sold out his right to be the god of this world to satan. Satan has the right to rule over us, but only until we become new creatures through the blood of Jesus Christ and come into the family of God. We are then rescued from the authority of darkness, and we are transferred into the Kingdom of God. That is why satan has no right to rule over believers or to dominate them. We need to have this revelation of truth inside of us to walk in the authority we have been given.

Satan, the god of this world is the head of all principalities, powers, and rulers of the darkness of this world. However, the power that is in us as believers of Jesus Christ is greater than the power that is in the world. The power that backs our authority, which is God, is greater than that which backs our enemies. We will never understand our authority with our intellect; it must be a revelation imparted to us by the Holy Spirit through reading scriptures.

Though we are in the world, we are not of the world. Satan may be influencing activity on earth, but he should not be influencing a believer of Jesus Christ. He should not dominate us; rather we should dominate him. We have authority over him. However, authority must be exercised upon the earth through a person who believes in Jesus Christ. Though Christ is not here in a physical body, He lives in those who believe in Him. We are now the body of Christ functioning on earth. It is ignorant to pray, asking the Lord to do something for us and just leave everything up to Him. He has conferred this authority to His body on earth; the Church.

We should not be moved by what we see, hear, or feel, but only by what we believe by the Word of God. Then we should stand on that Word. Many problems occur because we allow them to continue by being passive and not using our God-given authority.

Esther Had Authority

So, Queen Esther, daughter of Abihail, along with Mordecai the Jew, wrote with full authority to confirm this second letter concerning Purim.
Esther 9:29, NIV

God devised a plan to protect His people. He chose Esther to execute this protection by using legal authority. King Xerxes had authority in the land, but gave his authority to Esther who rewrote the laws in her land to provide protection for her people living there. She legally decreed life for her people preventing their annihilation. God has also assigned His Church to use authority through intercession, declarations, and decrees to speak life over our own lives, families, and territories.

Courageously, Esther boldly approached the king's throne. As she stepped out, the king held his golden scepter to her, which represented his authority, his rule, and his power. The king signified by this act that the same power he possessed was given to her over his entire empire. He extended his scepter signifying authority to her as she touched the scepter, which meant she accepted the authority he was giving to her to rewrite the laws governing her people.

With confidence, we can also come before the throne of our King to receive help for the things we need in our lives. We can receive a strategy and be granted the same authority Jesus had in the earth to carry it out. We can bring justice and reconciliation to our lives, our families, and into the territory, we are assigned to. However, we must know this authority belongs to us and act on it.

Let us then approach the throne of grace with confidence, so that we may receive mercy and find grace to help us in our time of need.
Hebrews 4:16, NIV

Esther found mercy and grace in her time of need. This is a benefit of living in the kingdom of God. Coming to God's throne, we make our requests known and find favor. Approaching Him with courage, we find God responsive to us when we need help. Esther found the king responsive to her, and that response saved all of the Jewish people in that day.

The rule of God's authority is for us. We only need to step up and take it. We can ask God for anything we want or need as long as it is aligned with His will, and expect to receive it. God says His power and authority is ours, which makes our prayers and declarations powerful. We need to have a great boldness overtake us through confidence in His Word. We must command destruction to be reversed, sickness to leave us, the enemy traps exposed, reverse judgments, and roadblocks and curses to be reversed. Esther took possession of the authority given to her, and she issued the command for her people to live and not be destroyed.

There should be a confidence that emanates from us when we pray. We should carry within us the same boldness today that Esther had in her day. Esther knew who she was, and showed respect and honor to the king. The confidence in her identity as queen and her love for her family and nation empowered her with the ability to speak with boldness and authority. She understood that if the king permitted her request, she had the authority to change a law that would save her people.

When the righteous thrive (are in authority) the people rejoice; when the wicked rule, the people groan.
Proverbs 29:2, NIV

If the righteous do not take this authority in their lives and in their land, the wicked will rise up, and governance will be oppressive causing the people to mourn. Those in authority must recognize the significance of their authority and steward it wisely to restrain evil so people can live in safety and prosper in their lives.

Similarly, within a family, parents have authority in their home to protect their family from harm so they can grow up in a secure and safe environment. When those in authority misuse their delegated oversight they have over others, it removes power from them. Children raised in a home where parents are abusive will feel powerless to govern themselves because a righteous authority is not imparted to them.[30]

We were intended to govern ourselves, and make wise choices for our lives, however, if the people in authority over us in our homes abuse that power, then we will not have godly power transmitted or imparted to us. Instead, the power to govern ourselves rightly will be removed from us.

When a child feels powerless, he will be unable to defend himself or to accomplish great things because he was made to feel that he didn't have the ability to accomplish great things. When we are made to feel powerless, the authoritative power God meant for us to have imparted into us, will instead be replaced by negative emotions such as fear, anger, rage, jealousy, envy, wrath, manipulation, control, hatred, and even murder. The abuse of the father's power over his children, makes the child feel powerless and helpless. It distorts their ability to govern their lives well. The person who is the head of a household has authority in their own house, but not everyone utilizes it correctly. Abuse of authority causes extreme damage to the family.

The good news is people can say *no* to the negative words

and harmful actions in the world that are not beneficial to them.

We do not have to receive words that are negative or false regarding who we are. We do not have to partake of or agree with actions that do not line up with the truth. We can say *no* to the people who do not celebrate us or bring out the good qualities that are in us. We can set boundaries in our relationships and even separate ourselves from the people who are not healthy for us to be around.

We can say *no* to sickness and poverty in our lives and put our trust in God to sustain us. This is having authority and using it. Through this relationship with God, reading Scripture and communicating with Him, we can discover all of the promises that belong to us, in order to govern ourselves rightly, using the authority given to us when we come into God's family.

When we have confidence in our God-given identity and authority, a boldness will come from us. We have the ability to command evil spirits to leave us and others so that bondages can be broken from off of us, sickness can be healed, and diseases have no place in our bodies. We can command evil words and actions to cease, and enemy traps to be exposed, and situations to become favorable for us. We can command roadblocks to be removed. God has extended to us the royal scepter like King Xerxes did for Esther, to take hold of and to rule and to reign in this life. Believers have been given this authority to exercise without any fear and without any intimidation.

The people were astonished at Jesus' doctrine because His words had authority.

Authority

All the people were amazed and said to each other, "What is this teaching? With authority and power, he gives orders to evil spirits and they come out!

Luke 4:36, NIV

Jesus' words were forceful. He spoke with confidence and with power. He was never negative. He spoke against demonic powers. He gave commands to demons and did not take commands from them. He told demons to go and they went. Kings talk differently than a common man talks. They speak with confidence and with authority.

The words that Jesus spoke were spirit and life. They were infused with the power and anointing of the Holy Spirit.

We are successor kings born into God's family, and we have His DNA in us. We should speak like a king speaks. We must speak like His successors and heirs speak. We must exercise kingdom jurisdiction and speak words that are alive and powerful.

When the apostles were threatened by the religious leaders in the city the apostles prayed for more boldness. The religious leaders threatened to put them in jail and do whatever they needed to do to keep the apostles from teaching about Jesus and from praying for the sick. They did not stop or back down, they were not passive but instead, they asked for even more boldness to use the authority they had been given.

Now Lord, consider their threats and enable your servants to speak your word with great boldness.

Acts 4:29, NIV

Five Smooth Stones

Boldness means to be frank, outspoken, command, order, and show freedom and confidence to speak. The apostles understood how they spoke really did matter and they did not want to allow passivity in their voices.

Just as the apostles prayed for God to give them the ability to stand as generals in their lives, we should stand as generals in our lives also. God confirmed their bold faith with bold language, signs, wonders, and miracles. It's no different in our lives today. This scripture is a description of bold language.

> *Thou shalt also decree a thing and it shall be established unto thee and the light shall shine upon thy ways.*
>
> Job 22:28, KJV

The lost are found, the sick are made whole, and those in bondage are set free when the righteous rule and reign, not when those with authority are passive and defeated. God gave the believer authority over sin, sickness, demons, poverty, addictions, and every disease.

When believers do not use their authority, the people perish. If a believer does not know their identity and walk in their authority, they will not overcome the things of this world.

David was the only one in all of Israel's army that had courage and boldness to accept Goliath's challenge. David knew who his God was, and that he had authority over anyone who made fun of his God. All of Israel was spared because of David's boldness and authoritative ability to slay the voice of intimidation. If David had been unwilling to courageously step out, the voice of intimidation would have won that day so that another nation could have taken all of Israel captive.

We must exercise authoritative language for salvation, deliverance, and healing to occur. We cannot deliver an uncertain sound and expect change. We are no longer slaves to be quieted under passivity. Silence is the worst negativity to give to other people. Negativity and passivity are uncertain sounds. Jesus said we should speak the same things the Father speaks, with authority. It is time to arise with boldness, and issue decrees of authority. God wants His people to speak with a voice of authority to overcome intimidation.

Queen Esther had a good relationship with her king. David had a good relationship with his Shepherd.

We too must have a good relationship with God to be secure in the authority He gives us. Relationship comes through familiarity and intimacy. We cannot have authority through passive relationships.

We need the Holy Spirit's help to receive and live in the authority God has given us. The Word and the Spirit agree. From reading Scripture, we know our authority comes from God, but it is manifested or demonstrated through the Holy Spirit abiding within us. The Holy Spirit and the Word are in agreement with what Father God says and does. We need both the Holy Spirit and the Word to slay intimidation.

For there are three that bear record in heaven, the Father, the Word, and the Holy Ghost: and these three are one.
1 John 5:7, KJV

Five Smooth Stones

Authority becomes ours at the time we give our lives to God because He becomes our Father and all that belongs to Him belongs to us. Jesus Christ defeated satan by dying on the cross, going to hell and taking back the keys of the Kingdom of God in the earth that Adam forfeited when he disobeyed God in the Garden. We activate this authority when we speak out God's will in prayers of intercession, declarations, and decrees. In order to do this properly, we need to become familiar with the Bible so we know what the heart, will, and mind of God is.

The Baptism of the Holy Spirit is available for every believer and gives believers the power to be a witness of the gospel of Christ Jesus. With this baptism, we receive a prayer language called tongues that enables our spirit to communicate directly to God and He to us. We also receive gifts and manifestations with the Baptism of the Holy Spirit. The gifts of the Spirit flow out of this communication and relationship with the heart and mind of God. We receive authority that is based on love and righteousness, which overcomes all the power of evil and darkness.

To fully take up and activate this smooth stone of Authority you should receive the Baptism of the Holy Spirit.

On one occasion, while he was eating with them, he gave them this command: "Do not leave Jerusalem but wait for the gift my Father promised, which you have heard me speak about. For John baptized with water, but in a few days, you will be baptized with the Holy Spirit.
Acts 1:4, 5, NIV

In the above passage, Jesus was telling the disciples that they were not to leave Jerusalem until they received the Baptism of the Holy Ghost. There was a reason they needed this Baptism of the Holy Spirit.

But you will receive power when the Holy Spirit comes on you, and you will be my witnesses in Jerusalem, and in all Judea and Samaria, and to the ends of the earth.
Acts 1:8, NIV

Jesus told the disciples to wait in the upper room until the Holy Spirit came and gave them power. The word power in this scripture means *ability; miracle; ruler, an extended meaning of a person or supernatural being who has administrative power; mighty works, miracles, strength, powers, might, virtue, mighty deeds, violence, wonderful works, and workers of miracles.*[31]

When Jesus ascended into Heaven the Holy Spirit came to earth so we would not be left alone. The Holy Spirit could not come to earth until Jesus was taken up into Heaven. God promised not to leave us alone here on earth.

First, He sent His son, Jesus, in human form so we could see what God the Father looked like and acted like in human form. When Jesus left earth, the Holy Spirit was able to come and be with us. He is our comforter, helper, counselor, teacher and helps us pray and much more. We only have to ask Jesus to baptize us with the Holy Spirit and receive Him by faith, just like those who waited in the upper room for the Holy Spirit to come upon them. When the Holy Spirit did come upon those waiting in

Five Smooth Stones

the upper room, they received a power to be witnesses.

A person receives Jesus Christ into their life by faith, and faith is activated by speaking. It is also by faith a person receives the baptism of the Holy Spirit. There is an authoritative power imparted to the person who receives this Holy Spirit baptism. With the Holy Spirit comes seeds of good fruit for our lives.

But the fruit of the Spirit is love, joy, peace, patience, kindness, goodness, faithfulness, gentleness, and self- control. Against such things, there is no law.
Galatians 5:22, 23, NIV

The baptism of the Holy Spirit also brings a release of the gifts within this person.

To one there is given through the Spirit the message of wisdom, to another the message of knowledge by means of the same Spirit, to another faith by the same Spirit, to another gifts of healing by that one Spirit, to another miraculous powers, to another prophecy, to another distinguishing between spirits, to another speaking in different kinds of tongues, and to still another the interpretation of tongues.
1 Corinthians 12:8-10, NIV

If you didn't know there was a baptism of the Holy Spirit, it would be helpful to read all of the Book of Acts and ask the Holy Spirit to help you understand what is being said in it. The believers in Ephesus had not heard yet about the Holy Spirit either.

Authority

...and asked them, "Did you receive the Holy Spirit when you believed?" They answered, "No, we have not even heard that there is a Holy Spirit."

Acts 19:2, NIV

Paul asked them what baptism they received and they replied John's baptism of repentance. John's baptism is full immersion water baptism after a person believes and receives Jesus Christ as their savior and Lord.

Paul said, "John's baptism was a baptism of repentance. He told the people to believe in the one coming after him that is, in Jesus."

Acts 19:4. NIV

Believers in Christ have a right and privilege to receive the Baptism of the Holy Spirit including a heavenly language. The Baptism of the Holy Spirit is available for all who believe in the Lord Jesus Christ. God does not respect just certain people but is a Father to all who love and receive Him.

On hearing this, they were baptized into the name of the Lord Jesus. When Paul placed his hands on them, the Holy Spirit came on them and they spoke in tongues and prophesied.

Acts 19:5, 6, NIV

Nobody needs to lay hands on us to receive the Baptism of the Holy Spirit. Sometimes it increases faith if hands are laid upon the person receiving, but it is not necessary. Jesus is the one who baptizes us, which means to immerse or wash over us with the Holy Spirit.

Five Smooth Stones

I would not have known him except that the one who sent me to baptize with water told me. The man on whom you see the Spirit come down and remain is he who will baptize with the Holy Spirit. I have seen and I testify that this is the Son of God.

John 1:33, 34, NIV

So, that we can receive this second smooth stone at the water brook we are going to ask Jesus Christ our Savior to baptize us with the Holy Spirit. The Holy Spirit empowers us to walk in the Authority we were meant to have. Would you pray this with me?

Lord Jesus, I ask you right now to baptize me with your precious Holy Spirit. When you rose to heaven you sent the Comforter, the Helper, the Counselor, the Holy Spirit to be with me on earth. I want to have this same Holy Spirit indwelling in me with the evidence of speaking in tongues. I ask you for this gift that you promised to give me.

Now believe and receive this gift of Holy Spirit. Release a sound from your belly; your language flows from there. It does not come from your head it comes from your belly. Stay in this place until you have a release of sound bubbling up from your belly. It becomes activated in your life, by speaking it out.

As a small child in the natural learns and speaks one word at a time and develops his speech we do the same in our spirit language. We may have just one sound that comes out of our belly and that is okay. It's our spirit speaking to God. Keep using and exercising this language and it will become more fluent. We can use our prayer language anytime to talk directly to Father God. He will help us to interpret and understand it. Use this prayer language every day to build a close relationship with God.

Take up the Smooth Stone of Authority

Thank you, Jesus for baptizing me in the Holy Spirit and for the evidence of speaking in tongues. My body is the temple of the Holy Spirit. It is the home in which the Holy Spirit dwells. I desire to think on your Word and talk with You every day. Show me how to honor You with my body and help me to pray. I take up this smooth stone of Authority and power to be a witness of your love.

Do you not know that your body is a temple of the Holy Spirit, who is in you, whom you have received from God? You are not your own, you were bought at a price. Therefore, honor God with your body.
                                                    1 Corinthians 6:19, NIV

Take up this smooth stone of *Authority* out of the water brook and remove the clay that covered it over. Receive the Baptism of the Holy Spirit to activate this authority God has given us. Read the study manual, the Bible, so we can know the policies and procedures. This is God's Word, His will, and His way for us to live our life. Our prayer language should be used every day to keep it activated in our life. Thank you, Father, for giving us all *Authority*.

Now we have the stones of *Identity* and *Authority*. Reading our Bible and talking to God daily will keep these stones smooth and polished. They are a most treasured gift from our heavenly Father who loves us.

Five Smooth Stones

No man or woman can fulfill their purpose on earth without overcoming intimidation and fear. David not only quieted this voice of intimidation that wanted to take a whole nation into bondage, but he cut off Goliath's head so the voice would never rise up again. That is acting aggressively toward the voice of intimidation! Let's be aggressive like that toward intimidation!

We have three more smooth stones to gather into our possession. The next smooth stone we will uncover is Love. Come with me on this journey along God's water brook and we will discover this smooth stone of *Love.*

Authority

Questions

1. What does authority mean?

2. Provide some examples of people who or positions that have authority.

3. What is the purpose that these people or positions are given authority?

4. What kind of fruit do we see in families when authority is not imparted to the children?

5. How much authority did Jesus have? How much authority do we have?

6. What are some things that take authority away from us?

7. Why do these things remove authority from us?

8. What is the result when the righteous use their authority?

9. What is the result when the righteous do not use their authority?

10. In what ways can we receive authority in our lives?

11. What is the power behind authority in a Christian's life?

12. What types of things does the Christian have authority over?

14. What do we receive when we are baptized in the Holy Spirit?

Five Smooth Stones

Thoughts

Is there a fire burning in you since you received the Baptism of the Holy Spirit?

What can you do to cause it to burn brighter?

5

Love

Let's sort through the rocks and find the smooth stone; *Love*.

The definition of love is *a deep and tender feeling of affection for or attachment or devotion to a person or persons. An expression of one's love or affection. A feeling of brotherhood and good will toward other people. A strong liking for or interest in something. The object of such liking. A strong, usually passionate, affection of one person for another, based in part on sexual attraction. The person who is the object of such an affection; sweetheart; lover. God's tender regard and concern for all human beings. Devotion to and desire to God as the supreme good that all human beings have.*[32]

That is Webster's definition, but let's look at the Bible's definition of love. It mentions the attributes of what love looks like, and how it should manifest in us. This definition gives us actions by which we can measure ourselves to determine how much love we really have working inside of us. We say we love people, but do we really? How full is our love tank compared to these characteristics?

Five Smooth Stones

Love is patient, love is kind. It does not envy, it does not boast, it is not proud. It is not rude it is not self-seeking; it is not easily angered; it keeps no record of wrongs. Love does not delight in evil but rejoices with the truth. It always protects, always trusts, always hopes, always persevere."
1 Corinthians 13:4-7, NIV

God designed four different types or levels of love. The first one is *storge*. This refers to a type of family love commonly found in the Bible and is vital to the proper functioning of families and extended families as well.

This is the type of love displayed between Martha and Mary who lost their brother Lazarus. This type of love is the same love Abraham felt for his son Jacob, that Noah shared with his wife and children and the love that any father or mother carries for their children.

Storge love can also occur between a husband and wife, as well as the children's love for their parents. It appears to be reflected in the form of attachment that animal parents seem to display for their young. *Storge* is the Greek word στοργή for family love and frequently used for natural affection.[33]

Be devoted to one another in brotherly love, Honor one another above yourselves.
Romans 12:10, NIV

This type of family love is unusually difficult to find based on the fact that only 50 percent of homes in our nation are two-parent homes. In 2014, 46 percent of the homes with children

Love

had two parents in a first marriage. Another 15 percent of the homes with children had two parents in a second marriage, 7 percent of the homes with children had adults that were cohabitating. Children in homes with only one parent accounted for 26 percent of the households in the United States.[34] These statistics reveal love is lacking in the home.

In God's kingdom of animals, many animals mate for life such as the Gibbon ape, wolves, termites, coyotes, barn owls, beavers, geese, crows, bald eagles, otters, macaw birds, orcas, lobsters, golden eagles, condors, swans, brolga cranes, French angelfish, Sandhill cranes, pigeons, prions, red-tailed hawks, red fox, titi monkeys, angelfish, ospreys, prairie voles, black vultures, lovebirds, seahorses, and the Quaker parrot. 90 percnet of all birds mate for life.[35] In contrast to humans, statistics show that the members of the animal kingdom are more committed to one another than the human species!

Eros is the another type of love. This word depicts the erotic love between men and women; a sensual love. It is acceptable within the confines of marriage, but outside of this matrimonial union, it is sinful. This is why Paul told the Corinthians it is better to marry within this form of love than to be with passion outside of marriage. This display of love gets many people, even Christians, into serious trouble because they may commit adultery if this type of love is left unchecked. If not, resisted they can commit adultery in the heart.

But if they cannot control themselves, they should marry, for it is better to marry than to burn with passion.
1 Corinthians 7:9, NIV

Five Smooth Stones

But I tell you that anyone who looks at a woman lustfully has already committed adultery with her in his heart.
                                                    Matthew 5:28, NIV

When this *Eros* love is unmet, it can lead to an addiction to pornography and become an idol in itself. While this type of love is necessary and healthy within marriage, outside or before marriage it is totally destructive. We have to know how to demonstrate self-control of our emotions and displays of affection for those of the opposite sex so we do not cross personal boundaries that lead us into sin. This kind of love should not be awakened until marriage or else it may be more difficult to manage in a person's life.

Another type of love is *Philia*. David and Jonathan shared this form of love. It is a committed selfless type of love, as love can be, outside of the love that God displays. These two men would have died for one other. This love produces a bond that *Eros* and *Storge* love cannot compare with. This is the love that Christians are commanded to have for one another.

My command is this: Love each other as I have loved you. Greater love has no one than this that he lay down his life for his friends.
                                                    John 15:12-13, NIV

Totally unselfish, *Philia* love reflects the love that soldiers display while under fire trying to save a fellow soldier who is wounded. During combat when a soldier falls on a grenade to save the life of his fellow soldiers, or when someone dies or risks their own life for another in order to save them, are examples of the sacrificial love *Philia* represents.

Agape is the form of love in the Bible. This is the supreme love of all and is an actual attribute of God. This love does not come naturally to humans. *Agape* is the supernatural display of love by Jesus on the cross. This is what Jesus said while dying on the cross for the sins of man.

Jesus said, "Father, forgive them for they do not know what they are doing.
Luke 23:34a, NIV

Agape is not so much a noun or an emotion felt, but it is an action displayed. *Agape* love is a verb; an action. Love is something we do. This type of love was displayed when Jesus died for us while we were still sinners. This action of *Agape* love is summed up in Romans 5:7-8. Not many people would die for their enemies or someone who does not care about them, but Jesus did.

Very rarely will anyone die for a righteous man, though for a good man someone might possibly dare to die. But God demonstrates his own love for us in this: While we were still sinners, Christ died for us.
Romans 5:7-8, NIV

This is not a love that condemned us, but one that came into the world to save us. It is interesting that the greatest commandment Jesus issued is all about love, loving God first, then our neighbor as ourselves. Loving God first means we seek

Five Smooth Stones

Him, His kingdom and His agenda above our own. Loving our neighbor is all about helping one another and looking out for each other's best interests.

It has nothing to do with gossiping and talking negatively about our neighbor. Our neighbor is anyone who is around us or anyone who we know. This kind of love is all about loving ourself also. There is only one person like ourself. It has been said that there are no two snowflakes alike in all the snow that falls on the earth. We were each designed by God and there is not another person made like us.

For God did not send his Son into the world to condemn the world, but to save the world through him.
John 3:17, NIV

When we place God first, our neighbors second, and ourselves last, we are demonstrating His commandments. It is on these two commands to love, that the entire message of the Bible is based. When we practice these two commandments in our lives, we are keeping all ten of the commandments in the Old Testament. When the disciples asked Jesus which was the greatest commandment, Jesus replied,

Jesus replied: "Love the Lord your God with all your heart and with all your soul and with all your mind. This is the first and greatest commandment. And the second is like it: 'Love your neighbor as yourself.' All the Law and the Prophets hang on these two commandments.
Matthew 22:37-40, NIV

God is very clear that the spirit He put within us is not the spirit of fear, but the spirit of love. We have not been given a spirit of fear, but God gave us a spirit of power, and of love, and of a sound mind. He also made it clear that partnering with the spirit of love was a way to displace fear in our lives. John wrote there is no fear in love, but perfect love casts out fear because fear has to do with punishment.

There is no fear in love. But perfect love drives out fear because fear has to do with punishment. The one who fears is not made perfect in love.
1 John 4:18, NIV

The one who fears is not made perfect in love.

When we are completed in love, fear cannot abide. When love is allowed to come in, it will push the fear out! To partner with the Holy Spirit, we must have a no tolerance policy for fear or punishment in our life and in our relationships. It doesn't matter how long fear has been in our lives, it can still be displaced by love. It requires letting go of offenses, anger, disappointment, and everything that is negative to allow love to fill up our heart.

We have to make a decision to partner with love and to make powerful choices. Powerful choices are to clear up any offenses that we may have against anyone and choose to love them instead. Choosing to think the best about everyone is how we keep our love active and prevent it from stopping.

Keeping love active is a heart condition. No person can

Five Smooth Stones

make us love or stop us from loving. In order to truly love the people around us, we must be open and vulnerable to them. Even if we are rejected or not treated in return with the same kind of love, we offer others, we must continue to remain open and vulnerable to others. Love is a force that has life in it. Once this force begins to build momentum in our lives after practicing loving others, we will be able to love fully and remove fear and intimidation and its effects. Keeping our love turned on creates fearlessness and deep vulnerability.[36]

Fear and love come from two opposing kingdoms. Fear comes from the devil, who would like nothing more than to keep people permanently disconnected and isolated. Love comes from God who is always working to heal and to restore man's connection with Him and with others to experience healthy life-giving relationships.

Confident people grounded in love can consistently be who they say they are. They know how to be themselves and invite those around them to be themselves also. This type of person is safe to be with because they allow others the freedom to be themselves. This is what love does.

In order to preserve relationships, one must learn to respond, instead of reacting to fear and pain. Responding does not come naturally, but is learned through practice. Responding with love in the face of pain and fear is essential for building healthy relationships. This practice will eventually become automatic and love will begin to take root in our minds and hearts.

Fear and love have opposite agendas and opposite strategies. They cannot coexist in a person, in a relationship, or even coexist in culture without conflict. Those who are free from fear are powerful people, and not slaves to their instincts. Powerful people have the ability to respond in a loving manner.

If we want to remove fear from our relationships, we cannot doubt in our mind and heart that we are truly loved. First, we must know without a doubt that God loves us and values us. Second, we can be confident enough in the fact that we are loved and that we can share our love giving it away to others. When we do this, we can change the atmosphere in our environment.

Each display of love, no matter how small, is a powerful act of spiritual warfare that removes anxiety from the environment and replaces it with freedom and safety. This invites each person to extend their best self forward in the relationship.

We communicate love by providing people with honest, relevant information about how their behavior affects their lives. A powerful person's choice to love will stand no matter what the other person does or says.

When powerful people say "I love you" there is nothing that can stop them.

Their love is not dependent on being loved in return. It is dependent on their constant choice to say *yes* and carry out that decision to love. A healthy relationship can only be built when people choose to love each other and take full responsibility for that choice. This choice must be based on who they are, what they want, and what they are committed to doing individually, to support their relationship.

Agape love says, "I will love you. I will protect you. I will serve you. I will be faithful to you, no matter what."

The foundation of true, lasting relationship is the decision that, "I choose to love you."

Love is the foundation for God's relationship with us.

You did not choose Me, but I chose you and appointed you to go and bear fruit-fruit that will last. Then the Father will give you whatever you ask in my name. This is my command: Love each other.
John 15:16, 17, NIV

Jesus chose us in the most difficult of circumstances. He chose us while we were in sin, while we were his enemies. His side of the relationship with us does not depend upon our choice, but entirely upon His choice. The question is whether or not we will learn to build our relationships with Him and others upon that same foundation of *Agape* love.

People with a foundation of love create a safe place to know and be known intimately. Relationships are protected by communicating and demonstrating love. Love requires communicating consistently in ways that people can hear and receive. Those who have grown up in a fear-based, love-starved relational culture, will find it revolutionary to break the silence and begin to actively communicate.[37]

God promises to help us communicate love to others.

I will instruct you and teach you in the way you should go; I will counsel you and watch over you.
Psalm 32:8, NIV

God leads us with his eyes and shows us how He feels about the choices we make and how they affect His heart. Eyes are the windows to the heart. When God shows us how our choices affect His heart we get to choose how we will respond. We will need to adjust to God's correction in order to protect our connection with Him. That is the real test of a healthy relationship. It is because of love.

Our success in walking in love and not in fear is fully determined by how powerful we are willing to become. Even when someone hurts us by their words or actions, we must not respond out of fear, pain, or rejection, but continue to exhibit the fruit of Love.

Not only so, but we also rejoice in our sufferings, because we know that suffering produces perseverance; perseverance, character; and character, hope. And hope does not disappoint us because God has poured out his love into our hearts by the Holy Spirit, whom he has given us.
Romans 5:3-5, NIV

Love is a seed planted in our hearts when we receive Jesus Christ as our Savior. It is a seed planted in us from the Spirit of God. It is up to us if we allow this seed to grow or not. This love

Five Smooth Stones

seed is allowed to grow in us as we forgive others. Love is like a fruit; it can grow or it can become stale and rotten. Each time we forgive, our fruit of love grows a little bigger, a little healthier and a little brighter.

This is how the smooth stone of *Love* is secured and activated, through forgiveness. There is no life apart from God's love. Therefore, there is no life apart from forgiveness. Forgiveness is the seal, the mark, and the proof of love. If we say we have love and cannot walk in forgiveness we deceive ourselves.

God knew that all of us, without exception, would be wronged. Furthermore, all of us will treat others in a wrong way. All of us sin against God and others. These sins block and hinder our relationship with Him. Jesus spoke more of forgiveness than possibly any other topic. This is a lesson we must learn on deeper levels until the very core of our being is changed into love.

Sin has destroyed far more than we realize. Only by Jesus' shed blood can we understand the extreme consequences of sin. God, in His mercy, has allowed us to see a small portion of the consequences of our sin in our lifetimes. We can change while we still have the opportunity. After we die it will be too late.

Love is the smooth pearl found in the sand that rubs against it. As a person forgives others from their heart, God will impart love and compassion. This love will easily overcome any voice of intimidation that rises up in a person's life.

In order to obtain and activate this smooth stone of *Love*, we must forgive everyone who has ever harmed us or offended us in any way. This removes the clay that covers the smooth stone of *Love*.

Let's pick up this smooth stone and wipe away all the debris from it so it will be useful to slay the voice of intimidation that wants to rise up against us. It is activated by forgiveness.

Let's pray a prayer of forgiveness together.

Take up the Smooth Stone of Love

Father, You said in Matthew 6:15, "But if you do not forgive men their sins your Father will not forgive your sins." Father, what they did to me was wrong and what they said about me was wrong and it hurt me very much. Father, I want to be free from the pain of this. I choose by an act of my will to not hold any grudge or unforgiveness towards them any longer. I want to be released from the pain and discomfort I feel inside when I think of them and that situation. I don't want to be connected to this pain anymore when I think about them or the situation. I want to release them from my heart.

So, Father, right now, I forgive them for what they did and for what they said and I release them to You and this whole matter into Your hands. I am released from the effects unforgiveness has on my mind, and on my heart, and on my body. It is in your hands Father. I give this matter over to you and ask that you would make things right.

I will pray for them when they come to my mind and I will choose to

Five Smooth Stones

be kind and to love them the way you do. Father when there is a situation that is unsafe for me to be around a certain person or persons that have ill will towards me, I will remove myself from that unhealthy relationship, into an environment where I am loved, appreciated, and celebrated. Help me discern and accept healthy kinds of relationships in my life. Help me to love You and to love others and to love myself. I take up this smooth stone of "Love" and I activate it in my life. Thank you, Father, for loving me.

We have now gathered from God's water brook the smooth stones of *Identity, Authority,* and *Love.* We are being equipped to slay the voice of intimidation that wants to rise up in our lives. Fear and intimidation cannot be overcome by our own strength we need to find this fourth smooth stone.

It will take God's *Grace,* working in us. The fourth smooth stone is *Grace.*

Let's discover *Grace* and how we can secure it in our lives.

Questions

1. What is a simple definition of love?

2. What is the Bible definition of love, and what does it look like?

3. What is the type of love that God has for us, and what does that look like?

4. What are some attributes of love in a marriage?

5. How do we get this love inside of us?

6. How do we allow this love inside of us to grow?

Thoughts

What can you do to increase love inside of you?

Five Smooth Stones

6

Grace

Let's look at Webster's Dictionary to get a basic definition of *Grace*. Then, we will go to the Bible and wade through the water of the Word to see how it applies to our lives.

Webster's definition of grace is: *a sense of what is right and proper; decency, thoughtfulness toward others; goodwill; favor; mercy, clemency; the unmerited love and favor of God toward human beings, divine influence acting in a person to make the person pure, morally secure, etc., the condition of a person brought to God's favor through this influence, a special virtue, gift, or help given to a person by God, to give or add grace or grace to; decorate; adorn; to bring honor to; dignity.*[38]

Grace is God's unearned favor. It is God's grace that gives us an ability to do something. He empowers us even when we feel mentally and physically weak. Each of us have talents and abilities, but ultimately it is God's grace that enables us.

We can abandon our efforts to hold everything together because it is not our responsibility to maintain everything. We only need to be who we are and rest in who He made us to be. We do not have to perform to be accepted or valued by God and should not perform to be accepted or appreciated by others. God isn't looking for performance. He only wants us to believe in, obey, and have a relationship with Him. God offers us grace and mercy to just come to Him and receive the help we need from

Five Smooth Stones

Him.

But he said to me, 'My grace is sufficient for you, for my power is made perfect in weakness.' Therefore, I will boast all the more gladly about my weaknesses, so that Christ's power may rest on me.
2 Corinthians 12:9, NIV

When Paul wrote in 2 Corinthians chapter 12, he shared how he was given many revelations and had vision encounters with heavenly things. However, there was no boasting or pride in Paul because of his astonishing revelations. Paul was in constant touch with his limitations because of a handicap or troubling circumstances. Paul experienced such difficulties that it brought him to his knees and in surrender to God, knowing he needed God's grace to survive. God told Paul His grace was enough and it was all Paul needed, Paul quit focusing on the troubling circumstances and relied on God's grace for the power that moved mountains for him.

Grace will be there to carry us through when we recognize that we are unable to accomplish things in our own strength. We too can ask for God's grace to cover us.

And God is able to make all grace abound to you, so that in all things at all times, having all that you need, you will abound in every good work.
2 Corinthians 9:8, NIV

We cannot earn our salvation; it is a gift. There is nothing we can do to earn God's grace; it too is a gift. We cannot do anything to earn a position with God or even with man. It is given to us when we receive Jesus Christ into our hearts and lives. That is grace! It is a gift we receive.

For it is by grace, you have been saved, through faith—and this not from yourselves, it is the gift of God.
Ephesians 2:8, NIV

We make a choice to receive God's gift of life through Jesus Christ, and it is a choice whether or not we will live according to His ways. Grace gives us the rightful position to be sons and daughters of the creator of the universe who promises to take care of us and to provide for us. It is by the grace and the goodness of God that makes us who and what we are.

But by the grace of God, I am what I am, and His grace to me was not without effect. No, I worked harder than all of them yet not I, but the grace of God that was with me.
1 Corinthians 15:10, NIV

God will put His grace on us to help us if we ask Him to. We labor in vain to become someone when we do it in our own strength. It is the grace of God with us that makes us who we are. We can put our trust in Him and not in our own abilities. As we apply our lives to His ways and His principles, He will make a way for us to prosper. The talents and abilities we have will work for us when we recognize that we have them by God's grace.

Because grace is such a healthy message, the enemy loves to dilute this message of grace, to distort it and to counterfeit it. This is why many different versions of grace are preached today.

Five Smooth Stones

Many people discover God's grace and conclude there are no more commandments. They sometimes believe that if Jesus Christ paid the debt of their sin, then it is okay to sin because it will be covered for them.

It may be that all blessings are given to us through the blood of Jesus, but obedience to God's word unlocks them. Blessings may be in our account, but they are not in our possession until there is an act of obedience or faith from us. It is God's grace that helps us to be obedient and to walk in faith.

Before Jesus died for our sins on the cross, God gave laws to the Israelite nation through Moses so they would know how to live. The commandments, or the law, required a particular lifestyle by which people should live. The very fact that the law exposed the truth meant that the Israelites could not keep it. God exposed the condition of humanity that needs a savior, and the only way that could be achieved was through a command the people could not keep.[39]

Even though we are unable to obey the law to the letter, it is established to give us guidance and boundaries. The law was designed to accomplish and perform. For example, the law says, "We shall not kill," but grace has a higher standard than the law. Grace says, "If you hate your brother, you have already murdered in your heart."

But I tell you that anyone who is angry with his brother will be subject to judgment.
Matthew 5:22a, NIV

Grace has a higher standard than the law. Instead, we act as if we are free to violate the law without consequence, and thereby misuse grace. When we have a law to obey, we are left trying to perform it, for instance, honoring our parents, or not taking anything that belongs to our neighbor. Grace brings a commandment that He enables us to perform.[40]

Grace says to honor our parents not only with our words and actions but with the motives and intents of our hearts. Grace says not to take anything that belongs to our neighbor, but also carries with it that we are to do good to our neighbors and help them whenever we can. Law has a standard that we meet a requirement. With grace, we start off accepted and are given the ability to live a victorious life. Grace works; it is not idle.

> *"You will be for me a kingdom of priests to me and a holy nation. These are the words you are to speak to the Israelites."*
> Exodus 19:6, NIV

Though God called the Israelites in the Old Testament to be holy, they chose the law instead of grace. Throughout history, people have rejected God's grace. God extended himself to all the nations in the world, but they rejected him by worshipping idols. Because of that, God took a seed of Abraham and raised up a nation called Israel. He displayed his love for them to provoke other nations to righteous jealousy and to let them know what was available to everyone. God showered His love on one nation to make it available to all nations. He called all of Israel to priesthood ministry, but Israel rejected this grace. Therefore, God took the tribe of Levi as a model to the rest of the nation to demonstrate what the entire nation was supposed to be.

Five Smooth Stones

Israel rejected the priesthood ministry. They chose rules instead of a relationship. They chose legalism instead of grace. They wanted Moses to talk to God and tell them what God was saying instead of talking to God for themselves. When the people saw the thunder, the lightning, heard the trumpet, and saw the mountain covered in smoke, they trembled with fear. They stayed at a distance.

The Israelites chose to live by written laws on a tablet signifying legalism, instead of walking and talking with God for themselves which demonstrated grace.

The people said, "Moses, you tell us what God is saying. We do not want to hear it first- hand. Tell us what to do and what not to do."

The people stayed at a distance, away from God.

When the people saw the thunder and lightning and heard the trumpet and saw the mountain in smoke, they trembled with fear. They stayed at a distance and said to Moses, "Speak to us yourself, and we will listen. However, do not have God speak to us or we will die."
Exodus 20:18, 19, NIV

They were afraid to come into relationship with God because they did not understand the grace God was offering to them. They came from Egypt where they lived by the law and did not know how to have a relationship by grace. This often happens in the lives of many believers. It is easier to have a list of what to do, and what not to do. However, grace is dependent upon relationship. Grace is dependent upon hearing the voice of God. Grace enables us to be all God calls us to be, but the law requires us to meet up to a certain standard.

Another example of grace is in Isaiah 58:6-9. This scripture describes at length the sacrifice of a true fast and all the wonderful benefits it accomplishes. When a person sets a fast, they abstain from eating certain foods or all foods for a specified period to seek God for an answer to a situation or purpose. A fast can even be abstaining from watching television or listening to technological devices. Fasting sets aside a particular time in the day to talk with God about a specific concern to get a breakthrough.

"Is not this the kind of fasting I have chosen: to loose the chains of injustice and untie the cords of the yoke, to set the oppressed free and break every yoke? Is it not to share your food with the hungry and to provide the poor wanderer with shelter when you see the naked to clothe him, and not to turn away from your own flesh and blood? Then your light will break forth like the dawn, and your healing will quickly appear; then your righteousness will go before you, and the glory of the Lord will be your rear guard. Then you will call, and the Lord will answer; you will cry for help, and he will say; Here am I. If you do away with the yoke of oppression, with the pointing finger and malicious talk . . .
Isaiah 58:6-9, NIV

"But go and learn what this means, I desire mercy, not sacrifice."
Matthew 9:13a, NIV

Five Smooth Stones

Though God says it takes grace to deny ourselves the things of the world, such as food or certain conveniences, it takes a greater grace to have compassion toward someone. We can skip a meal, but God is saying, let me show you what I want from you. He desires compassion from us above sacrifice. This takes a greater grace. We can sacrifice things in our lives, but God wants our hearts to be touched with compassion so we can affect the people around us. It takes grace to fast, but it takes a greater grace to have a heart of compassion. This compassion is a grace on us that will reset the moral compass in people's lives. Grace allows people to move with compassion above sacrifice and it empowers God's presence in our lives.

Grace empowers the presence of God in us to live as Jesus lived. It enables us to do the impossible. Grace does not empower us to sin or to overlook sin, but instead, it empowers us to obey, to walk according to the ways God has for us. It empowers us to be more efficient in service to others. The people we serve should benefit from the grace in our life. One such story about grace the life of Hezekiah.

Hezekiah restored worship, and all the other kings and nations paid tribute to the Lord and Hezekiah. He was much promoted and brought about transformation to an entire nation. Hezekiah's wisdom of God ignited leaders of other nations to desire that same wisdom. They brought gifts to Hezekiah and the Lord. He was indeed a reformer.

However, Hezekiah became sick, and cried out to God that he might live. So, God gave him fifteen more years. It was God's will to give Hezekiah these fifteen more years to live, but in that time, Hezekiah became arrogant in his riches, and the honor he received from other nations. This was not God's will. Thus, Hezekiah was miserable for those last fifteen years.

These additional years were added to Hezekiah's life due to God's grace. This was a gift from God and not something Hezekiah accomplished for himself. Hezekiah was unwilling to be thankful to God for the gift of grace he had been given to live fifteen more years. Hezekiah's arrogance and being unthankful during his last fifteen years was not the purpose of God.

Because of the grace Hezekiah received during his life, a more intentional acknowledgment of thankfulness towards God was required of him. Hezekiah failed to recognize he was given a large measure of grace in being honored by the kings of other nations. This was not something he accomplished on his own accord. Not only did he need to be thankful for God's grace and goodness on his life, but God required an offering that would cost Hezekiah something. The offering could be giving of his time in service to someone else or going out of his way in some manner to help another.

Hezekiah was surrounded by extreme favor, applause, and accolades. God wants us to have applause and accolades, but He does not want it to destroy us. We can become arrogant and take the credit for success when it is God's grace in our lives, and it has nothing to do with our greatness. God wants grace to drive us into an attitude of servanthood and discipleship by recognizing it is His grace on us. We cannot achieve anything in our own power. The more we are promoted, the more we must become intentional in giving God thanks and the glory for what He

Five Smooth Stones

accomplishes through us. We cannot fulfill our purpose on our own; it will require God's grace.

The world's view of promotion is a raise in pay and higher status in the company, which usually brings us into a position where we can no longer understand people's needs. As we ascend up the ladder in the secular world, we move from the conveyor line or storeroom into an office away from the people. We are promoted to a higher position that is usually farther away from the people. However, in the Kingdom of God, promotion puts us into dependence on God for the necessary resources and strength so we can best serve the people's needs. Therefore, we become closer in proximity to people, serving others at a more sacrificial level and with dependence on His grace in us.[41]

Another example of grace is 2 Samuel chapter 24. David committed a foolish sin by numbering his people to calculate whether they could battle their enemy. David was looking at the strength of his army. This was a sinful act because David was fearful and looking at his own strength, not relying on God to direct him.

Again, the anger of the Lord burned against Israel, and he incited David against them, saying, "Go and take a census of Israel and Judah.

2 Samuel 24:1, NIV

Sin has consequences. When God's grace enables us to overcome difficulties in our lives, there should be some acknowledgment we give to God in the form of thanks and sacrificial offering. This is an aspect of grace we misunderstand.

Grace

When God's grace is upon us, there should be some form of acknowledgment on our part that blesses other people. God's grace upon our lives was not meant for us to keep to ourselves, but to share with others.

As a consequence of David's sin, God gave him three options to choose from. The three consequences were to have three years of famine, three months of defeat by his enemies, or three days at the hand of the Lord. David's response was three days at the hand of the Lord because he knew the mercies of God were very great. He did not want to fall into the hands of man. David asked the Lord to remove the consequence, and the Lord told him to make an offering, a sacrifice, on Araunah, the Jebusite's property. Araunah told David he could have the property, and oxen for the sacrifice, and wood to burn on the altar. Araunah told David to take all of it and give it to God in a sacrifice. However, David responded in 2 Samuel 24:24 that he wanted to buy the property, the oxen, and the wood from Araunah. He said he would not give God something that didn't cost him something.

But the king replied to Araunah, "No, I insist on paying you for it. I will not sacrifice to the Lord my God burnt offerings that cost me nothing.
2 Samuel 24:24a, NIV

God showed grace to David. It still cost David the price of Araunah's oxen and property as a sacrifice for his sin of not trusting God to help him win the battle against his enemies, even though God had always helped him in the past. David counted the number of men in his army because he was fearful.

Five Smooth Stones

This was the real test that David had to face, his fear. Grace overcomes fear.

God's grace would have helped David win the battle against his enemy no matter how many were in his army. These are encounters of grace!

God's grace enables us to have encounters with Him in various ways. One of those is in having visions and hearing His voice. Peter fell into a trance while praying on a rooftop. A trance is a half-conscious state. He was tired from traveling, and while praying, he went into a half-conscious state. The Lord spoke to him in a vision during this time. After this, the Lord told Peter to go with the three men to Cornelius' house. Peter was sent there to share the message of the gospel; the gift of the Holy Spirit was poured out on all the Gentiles. It is God's grace that comes on us to have encounters with Him. He (Peter) became hungry and wanted something to eat, and while the meal was being prepared, he fell into a trance.

Acts 10:10, NIV

Paul also fell into a trance while praying. During this time, he saw the Lord speaking to him. The Lord warned Paul to leave Jerusalem right away because the people were not going to receive him, and therefore, his life was in danger. It is the grace of God that speaks to us and shows us eminent danger so that He can help us. It is grace that while we are praying that we can see visions and hear God's voice clearly.

When I returned to Jerusalem and was praying at the temple, I fell into a trance and saw the Lord speaking, "Quick! He said to me.

'Leave Jerusalem immediately, because they will not accept your testimony about me.

Acts 22:17, 18, NIV

Evangelist Mary Woodworth-Etter went into trances and stood motionless for hours and sometimes for days. In the Bible, trances were primarily connected to prayer and intercession. This is partly due to the humility of heart brought about by this kind of devotion.[42] But He gives us more grace. That is why scripture says;

God opposes the proud but gives grace to the humble.

James 4:6, NIV

God shows grace to the humble. Prideful people do not need grace because they receive their honor from man. That is why much grace is given to the humble. The humble give the honor and the glory back to God. They recognize nothing in themselves can change difficult circumstances. Only through the grace of God can things change. It is nearly impossible to maintain a humble prayer life, and not encounter the supernatural on one level or another. It is God's grace that enables this.

The kindness of the Lord is intended to provoke humility, dependency, and sacrifice from every believer.

We do not repay God; we cannot even afford to pay Him. Nothing we can do will pay God for His kindness in speaking to us or taking time to talk to us. Nothing you and I can do through our own goodness, sacrifice, or anything can cause Him to speak to us. It is simply His grace.

Five Smooth Stones

Grace does not make sense to our natural minds; it is a mystery. It is the Holy Ghost that performs God's grace in us and through us. He who made the promise has the responsibility of keeping the promise. God who promises this marvelous change, will assuredly carry it out in all who receive Jesus. We only need to trust in his grace to give us a new heart, and a right spirit! This is accomplished by grace.

I will give them an undivided heart and put a new spirit in them; I will remove from them their heart of stone and give them a heart of flesh.

Ezekiel 11:19, NIV

The foundation of our salvation is the grace of God. Because God is gracious, sinful men are forgiven, converted, purified, and saved. It is not because of anything in man that they are saved. It is only the boundless love, goodness, pity, compassion, mercy, and grace of God.

God knows that we cannot change our own hearts nor can we change our own nature. God knows that He can do both. God can even create us a second time by causing us to be born again. This is a miracle of grace, which only the Holy Ghost can perform.

Grace is a gift we receive from God, but it can be lost. When we drift away from our relationship and dependence on God, we will fall away from grace. When we fall away from having an intimate relationship with Jesus Christ, we fall away from grace. Then, we begin to live within the boundaries of the law. We are no longer led by the Holy Spirit, but by our natural senses apart from God's grace.

> *You who are trying to be justified by law have been alienated from Christ; you have fallen away from grace.*
> Galatians 5:4, NIV

How then can we secure, protect and activate this fourth smooth stone of Grace that helps to defeat the spirit of intimidation?

We need to return to our intimate relationship with Jesus Christ and not be led by the desires of our flesh. We are spirit beings in a covenant with God through the blood of Jesus Christ and should be led by the Holy Spirit. This will bring us back under God's grace.

> *So, I say live by the Spirit, and you will not gratify the desires of the sinful nature.*
> Galatians 5:16, NIV

Being led by the Holy Spirit, we have the grace to overcome obstacles in life. Being led by our carnal nature, we will suffer many difficulties. These scriptures continue to tell us what is manifested in our lives when we live in our flesh, our sensual nature, and not by the Holy Spirit.

Five Smooth Stones

The acts of the sinful nature are obvious: sexual immorality, impurity, and debauchery; idolatry and witchcraft; hatred, discord, jealousy, fits of rage, selfish ambition, dissensions, factions, and envy; drunkenness, orgies, and the like. I warn you, as I did before, that those who live like this will not inherit the kingdom of God.

Galatians 5:19, NIV

When we live by the Spirit of God, we will have the fruit of the Spirit manifesting in us. It is easy to discern how people are living based on the fruit they are manifesting. They are either living according to their own nature, which is sin, or they are living by the leading of the Holy Spirit. These fruits and attributes of the Holy Spirit are given to us by God's great grace.

But the fruit of the Spirit is love, joy, peace, patience, kindness, goodness, faithfulness, gentleness, and self-control. Against such things, there is no law. Those who belong to Christ Jesus have crucified the sinful nature with its passions and desires. Since we live by the Spirit, let us keep in step with the Spirit.

Galatians 5:22-25, NIV

The fourth smooth stone of *Grace* is secured by being led of the Spirit of God and not fulfilling the deeds of the flesh. Let's pick up this fourth smooth stone of *Grace* and activate it in our lives by speaking this prayer.

Take up the Smooth Stone of Grace

Father, in the precious name of Jesus Christ, I turn away from all forms of sexual immorality, impurity, and debauchery; idolatry and witchcraft; hatred, discord, jealousy, fits of rage, selfish ambition, dissensions, factions, envy, drunkenness, orgies, and the like. I repent from all of my involvement with these activities. I renounce them in my life and choose to have no part of them.

I ask you, Father, for the fruit of the Spirit to be planted in my life. I will water this fruit by reading my Bible and talking to you during the day. Thank you for planting in me by Your grace the fruit of love, joy, peace, patience, kindness, goodness, faithfulness, gentleness, and self-control.

I want to be led by your Holy Spirit every day. I want to have your Grace and favor operating in my life, and no longer a legalistic mindset. I take up this smooth stone of Grace and activate it in my life by denouncing the ways of the flesh and purposing to be led by Your Holy Spirit. Thank you, Father, for your Grace.

Fear and intimidation cannot live in an environment of grace. When you have this fruit manifesting in you, there is no room for fear to dwell. It is choked out just like a weed is choked out of a beautiful flower garden.

We have secured four smooth stones that will enable us to slay the voice of intimidation in our lives. They are *Identity, Authority, Love,* and *Grace.*

The fifth smooth stone for us to obtain to defeat the enemy of Intimidation is *Humility*. Come and travel with me along the water brook of the Bible to search out this smooth stone of *Humility*.

Five Smooth Stones

Questions

1. What is a simple definition of grace?

2. Why was it hard for the Israelites to receive God's grace?

3. Why is having compassion greater than sacrifice?

4. Why was Hezekiah miserable in the last 15 years of his life?

5. What is the difference in relationships between God promoting man and the world promoting man?

6. Does man have any responsibility towards God when he by grace overcomes difficulty?

7. How do we maintain grace in our lives?

8. What are some of the fruits of the flesh?

9. What are some of the fruits of the spirit?

Thoughts

Is there anything God has brought you out of that you need to thank Him for?

7

Humility

Often, we skim through our days never considering there is something so simple as humility that can cause us to overcome a difficult situation. Humility is one of those valuable character qualities that will cause us to be established in a place of honor and good standing no matter what the situation is or who it involves.

The definition of humility according to Webster is *the state or quality of being humble; absence of vanity or excessive pride; showing respect, unassuming attitude, and behavior toward others, low in rank without pretentions or attempting to impress others*.[43]

Humility says no matter what my title or my position is, who I am or who I think I am, I can have an attitude of goodness and kindness toward you and serve you for your benefit and for your success.

When you know who you are in Christ and what you have to offer you will gladly give it away without getting any credit or glory.

Change My Ways

Early in my Christian walk, the Holy Spirit was incredibly

Five Smooth Stones

patient to show me just one sinful way that I was living at a time so I could deal with and remove it from my life. I asked God with a repentant heart to help me change those areas of my life that were not pleasing to Him because I desired to be as close to Him as I could. I knew He loved me and He wanted the best for me. I knew He wanted to remove certain sins, actions, and attitudes from me because they were unclean to Him, and it was advantageous for me.

God gave me something better to replace the unclean thing that was removed from me. I was happy to have this relationship with the Holy Spirit. He was not condemning toward me at all. He would shine His light in an area and then I would begin to search it out. I wanted to find scripture related to what He was showing me so I knew how to pray and how to be set free from it.

I did the best I could to make adjustments in my life and align with scripture. Amazingly, it seemed there would be a speaker in my area who offered a teaching on the very same subject I was changing in my life. Therefore, I received further deliverance in that area in exchange for what I gave up that was not good for me, I received joy, a feeling of freedom, a sense of being closer and more intimate with Him. Because of this process, I knew any righteousness I had was only from Him. No human person could have done this work in my heart like the Holy Spirit was doing for me.

Any holiness or righteousness I received, was truly a gift. Jesus Christ paid our debt of sin by going to Hell for us. We have no right or cause to have lofty thoughts that we can live here on earth without the person, Holy Spirit. There is nothing in us that has anything of value if God's signature is not on it. If a thought or action does not have God's smile on it, and if it doesn't give Him honor, then we shouldn't want it.

I didn't know I was seeking humility, I just desperately wanted to be rid of anything that He did not want me to have. It would only weigh me down and cause me to feel be separated from Him therefore, I was finding humility.

He is the Creator

Humility is not something that we bring to God or that He bestows on us. It is simply the sense of understanding a complete nothingness that comes when we see how God truly is all, and we make way for Him to be all. When we consent to have His will, mind, and affections in us, then we can be the vessel in which the life and glory of God are at work and manifested in us. We need to acknowledge the truth of our position as creature and yield to God His place as Creator.[44]

The fear of the Lord teaches a man wisdom, and humility comes before honor.
Proverbs 15:33, NIV

The believer who wants to pursue holiness in their life will come to understand what humility is. Humility will lead to a purity of character because Jesus will become everything and nothing else will matter. That believer will leave behind the ways of the world and the influence of the culture around them.

Five Smooth Stones

Price for Humility

There is a price to pay for humility. Christ bought it for us through His own death, burial, and resurrection. We purchase it the same way, by dying to our own desires and wants. We pay the price when we do not get offended when someone talks badly about us. When they hurt us, we choose to bless them with our words, and even with our finances. There is very little hope of a religion that will conquer the world without humility. It does not seek its own desires, but to serve others. Jesus did not lose anything by giving all to God. God honored His trust and did all for Him.

But made himself nothing, taking the very nature of a servant, being made in human likeness. And being found in appearance as a man, he humbled himself and became obedient to death, even death on a cross! Therefore, God exalted him to the highest place and gave him the name that is above every name.
Philippians 2:7-9, NIV

A Christian must present him or herself to God as one who has died in Christ, and in Christ is alive from the dead, bearing about in His body the dying of the Lord Jesus.

I often asked God, "How do I die to myself?"

I wanted to be dead to my own desires so that I could have His desires. I didn't realize the making of humility was in the very tests and difficulties I was going through at the time. I forgave over and over, but still felt anxiety over situations. I wanted to keep my heart right, but the pain and the brokenness inside of me did not go away for what seemed a long time. It seemed to be unrepairable.

Christ was betrayed, rejected, scorned, and beaten for no reason at all. He didn't ever harm anyone or do anything wrong. How do we think that our lives will be without any suffering if we love Him and want to be like Him?

The price of humility is walking in forgiveness, gentleness, kindness, longsuffering, and loving in the midst of jealousy and hatred. We have to learn to keep our hearts in a peaceful state even in the midst of chaos around us. Learning to lay down our offenses toward others is a must. Learning to pray for those who misuse us and treat them with the same kindness God treats us with, is also a must. This does not mean we allow people to walk over us and mistreat us without confronting circumstances and removing ourselves from hostile environments.

When proper boundaries are in place in our lives, our hearts can be healed of any wounding we endure. Humility will position us to have an upright attitude toward people and toward God so there will be no offense remaining in us.

The Pursuit of Humility

Every Christian is presented with choices to pursue humility. In the pursuit of humility, we will have a choice to either face the fear that presents itself or to flee from the fear of that which is causing us to be humbled. If we face the difficulty to walk through it correctly then we will learn humility. But if we flee from the difficulty then we are not delivered from the fear and intimidation of it.

Five Smooth Stones

Paul had a thorn in his flesh and asked to have it removed. Paul asked the Lord three times to have this thorn removed.

To keep me from becoming conceited because of these surpassingly great revelations, there was given me a thorn in my flesh, a messenger of Satan, to torment me. Three times I pleaded with the Lord to take it away from me.
2 Corinthians 12:7, 8, NIV

The answer came that the trial was a blessing. In the weakness and humiliation, it brought Paul grace and strength. This is the price that is paid for the character of humility.

In the pursuit of humility instead of enduring it, we need to be glad in it. Instead of asking for deliverance, we should take pleasure in it. This is where we learn that the place of humility can be the place of blessing, power, and joy. We should seek humility at any cost.

We pray for humility, but in our hearts, we pray more to be kept from the very things that make us humble. This only will prolong the process God wants to take us through to form us into His image.

Consider Others Above Yourself

The work of God in us is hindered because we have been touchy, hasty, impatient, self-defending, self-asserting, sharp in judgments, or use unkind words. We are to reckon others as better than ourselves. That does not mean we won't like ourselves but that we place a high value on other people. We are already accepted, loved, safe, secure, and dead to ourselves.

Humility

Other people need to see these same attributes in us. How or where else will others see what humility looks like?

Do nothing out of selfish ambition or vain conceit, but in humility consider others better than yourselves.
Philippians 2:3, NIV

In what we consider as being a holy person or a holy lifestyle, there is really little humility. May God teach us that our thoughts, words, and feelings concerning our fellow men are a test of our humility toward God and not the person.

Our humility before God is the only power that can enable us to always be humble with others. Our humility must be the life of Christ within us that is seen on the outside. This is eternal love humbling itself, clothing of meekness and gentleness, to win, serve, and save us. Christ in us, is humility embodied in human nature. This humility is available to us when we receive Jesus Christ as our Savior and allow Him to reconstruct our character nature.

The little things that happen in our daily lives are the tests of eternity because they prove what spirit possesses us. In our most unguarded moments, we really see what we are. We can know a humble man by how he behaves. We only need to follow a man in the course of his daily life and it will easily show how humble he is. Humility is nothing if it is not proven in daily life.

We should consider every person who tries or vexes us, as God's instrument for our purification. Not many homes, schools or mentors teach us how to allow vexing by others to purify us!

Five Smooth Stones

Difficulties can be the exercise of humility working in us. A humble man feels no jealousy or envy. He has lost himself in finding God.

The seasons of our lives when we are focused on finding God and knowing Him, can be the most rewarding and the most difficult. Our hearts will be tested as to how we will respond to being falsely accused, misunderstood, involved in legal issues, and all manner of situations and circumstances. There is no place in a person's heart for jealousy, or strife. If we are truly seeking God's presence nothing else matters except to be as close as we can to Him. There just isn't room for things that have no value. We should have no desire to compare ourselves with others because there is no value in that. It does not create good character in us.

It is a wonderful place to be, to give up every thought of self. When we do this, we take on a heart of compassion, kindness, humility, meekness, and long-suffering. When we are not so focused on our own desires, we can forbear one another and forgive one another just like the Lord forgave us.

I have been crucified with Christ and I no longer live, but Christ lives in me. The life I live in the body, I live by faith in the Son of God, who loved me and gave himself for me.
Galatians 2:20, NIV

The Greatest Among You Must Be a Servant of All

The Sermon on the Mount in Matthew opens with Jesus speaking about humility. His first words of the Kingdom of Heaven reveal the open gate through which we alone enter. The poor who have nothing in themselves, it is to them that the kingdom comes. To be poor, meek, and humble before God requires us to be repentant.

Humility recognizes God as the ruler of all and the one from whom all success and blessings come from. It recognizes Jesus as the only perfect and blameless one and it puts into perspective just how small we are and that we are only made great in Him. A right perspective will take our sight off ourselves and focus on God. God is love and love serves others. We walk in humility by serving others.

Blessed are the poor in spirit, for theirs is the kingdom of heaven.
Matthew 5:3, NIV

Blessed are the meek (humble) for they will inherit the earth.
Matthew 5:5, NIV

God described Moses as the humblest man on earth. It certainly does not mean he was the most financially lacking of all men. From his face-to-face encounter with the Lord on the mountain, he was undoubtedly the meekest and humblest man on earth.

The closer we are to God, the more humble we become. Look at the assignment God gave to Moses! Going before Pharaoh to tell him to let the Israelite people leave Egypt. When Pharaoh didn't let the people go, God sent ten plagues upon the land. Yet Moses didn't become arrogant as if he had any power or ability to cause this to happen. Instead, Moses became the humblest man on earth.

Five Smooth Stones

Now Moses was a very humble man, more humble than anyone else on the face of the earth.
                                                    Numbers 12:3, NIV

Humility is the secret blessing of heavenly and earthly life. Meekness and lowliness is the one thing He offers us. Few will want this, but in it is where we find perfect rest for our souls. A person with true humility has his roots deep into the grave of Jesus in the death of sin and self. However, he also has his head lifted up to the heavens by the resurrection power where Jesus is. Humility alone makes this inseparable connection between Heaven and Hell.[45]

We can rest in knowing who we are and that our value comes from having Jesus Christ living inside of us, instead of striving in our own strength to be someone we were never meant to be. Moses is the greatest example of humility. True humility gives total confidence and security in who God has made you.

Just as a small child is innocent and unguarded so is a person of humility. The baptism of humility, is the glory of Heaven. Whosoever is chief among you, let him be your servant. Humility allows you to know who you are and who God has created you to be

When we are secure in who we are, we can humble ourself to serve others.

Insecurity will cause us to wait for another to stumble or fall. It will look for fault or blame. True humility says I know what God has put inside of me and I know what I have to offer and because it came from Him and not me. I can give it freely with no expectation in return.

Not so with you. Instead, whoever wants to become great among you must be your servant, and whoever wants to be first must be your slave, just as the Son of Man did not come to be served, but to serve, and to give his life as a ransom for many.
Matthew 20:26-28, NIV

Humility is the only ladder to a place of honor in God's kingdom. The opposite is true in the kingdom of the world. To climb the ladder to a place of success and greatness commonly requires self-exaltation and striving.

If we could just learn that being nothing before God is our glory, then we can welcome the discipline of serving even those who try us or vex us. Just as water seeks to fill the lowest place, so the moment God finds us abased and empty, His glory and power flows in us. This is the path to the glory of Christ's presence in us, and His power resting on us.

Our one need should be humility. As the meek and lowly One, He will come in and dwell in the one who has this longing in their heart.

Take my yoke upon you and learn from me, for I am gentle and humble in heart, and you will find rest for your souls.
Matthew 11:29, NIV

For three years the disciples were in the training school of Jesus. He told them that He wished to teach them the chief

Five Smooth Stones

lesson. Time after time He spoke to them, to the Pharisees, and to the multitude, about humility as the only path to the glory of God. Jesus said he was one who serves. He washed their feet and told them they were to follow His example. Yet, it seemed to avail little.

Even at the Last Supper, there was still contention as to who should be the greatest. It is only when we truly know that we can do nothing of ourselves, that God will do all. Only when we grasp the reality that Christ by His Spirit truly lives inside of us, will we know humility.

Tests Develop Character

God brought the nation of Israel out of Egypt, then He fed them and took care of them for forty years. The people of Israel were learning to depend on God as their Father for their needs instead of themselves, or the government of Egypt. This was a test that lasted forty years in order to bring these people to a place of humility and dependence on God. It took forty years for these people to learn to be humble and depend on God for all their needs.

We hear this story and have a hard time believing they couldn't trust God after He just divided the Red Sea. However, we do not stop to realize we are living the same way now, going through those same tests, for the very same purposes.

The Israelites took a very long time to learn to depend on God. They saw the miracle of the Red Sea open, and, water come from the rock at Moriah, and food fall from heaven.

Humility

It is taking us the same amount of time for God to work those same lessons in our lives. I have to confess, it has taken me that long to even realize that the tests I was going through were meant to develop my character. I experienced many wonderful encounters along the way that I knew came from God, yet I still struggled with trusting God to help me.

We must pass the tests placed before us to develop and mature in humility before we can come out of that season. Our tests are not for nothing, but cultivate and develop humility in us. God in His kindness and redemptive abilities will use everything in our lives, the good, the bad, and the ugly, all for His glory.

Remember how the Lord your God led you all the way in the desert these forty years, to humble you and to test you in order to know what was in your heart, whether or not you would keep his commands. He humbled you, causing you to hunger and then feeding you with manna, which neither you nor your fathers had known, to teach you that man does not live on bread alone but on every word that comes from the mouth of the Lord.
Deuteronomy 8:2, 3, NIV

When we accepted Jesus Christ as our Savior and were baptized in the Holy Spirit, we died to ourselves and now He lives inside of us. We gave up our lives to allow Him to live through ours. We accepted His will and His desires for our lives and no longer our will and our desires. In order to work this out in us, we go through trials and tests removing pride from us. As we pass these trials and tests, we become humble and we become overcomers.

Five Smooth Stones

Consider it pure joy, my brothers, whenever you face trials of many kinds because you know that the testing of your faith develops perseverance. Perseverance must finish its work so that you may be mature and complete, not lacking anything.

James 1:2-4, NIV

The Attitude of Thankfulness

The people of Israel saw mighty displays of miracles and heavenly provision of food and water, yet most of them did not come to a place of humility. An attitude of thankfulness will be a fertilizer in the roots of humility. Recognize and do not take for granted the good things in your life. Keep the soil of your heart soft, and pliable so that it can grow good fruits of meekness and gratefulness.

Guard Your Heart

The lack of humility is the sufficient explanation of every defect and failure. Coming from a farming background I witnessed and experienced first-hand the laborious work of plowing the ground to prepare the soil so we could plant our crops. Rain and sun were required in the growing process so the seed could mature into a healthy plant producing much fruit. If the ground was not properly prepared, the seed would either die before it could grow or if it did grow the plant would not be strong. It is the same with our hearts.

When our hearts are plowed with humility, they are soft and produce good fruit in our lives. If the soil in our heart has not been properly prepared by humility, then the good seed will not take root in our lives and there may be a defect in our character that causes a measure of failure in our lives. Yet, as we make humility an object of special desire, prayer, faith, and practice, Jesus Christ himself will come to impart His humility in us.

Just like the farmer has to labor in the field to plow the ground, so a person will be required to labor over the soil of his heart with humility. Humility is a condition of the heart. That is why it is vital to know what is in our hearts and cultivate the soil of our hearts with humility.

The word of wisdom in Proverbs tells us to keep our heart with vigilance. Vigilance is defined as the action or state of keeping careful watch for possible danger or difficulties. All the issues of life are stored in our hearts. Our attitudes, thoughts, nature, words we speak that we didn't know were inside of us all come from deep within. We don't even know some of the things that are in our hearts, but God does. That is why God tells us to pay special attention to our hearts watching over. We watch over our hearts by talking to God about what is concerning us or how to deal with certain situations. As He counsels us through the Word and through conversation with Him, we can keep a right attitude toward others and handle our difficulties with wisdom.

Keep your heart with all vigilance, for from it flow the springs of life.
Proverbs 4:23, ESV

Give No Place to Pride

Something must be removed from us so humility can take its rightful place. It is pride. Pride goes before destruction, a

Five Smooth Stones

haughty spirit before a fall. Pride is the opposite of humility. We will either humble ourselves or God will do it for us. The latter is much more painful than the first. Even nations that are overly prideful God says He will bring an end.

When pride comes, then comes disgrace, but with humility comes wisdom.
Proverbs 11:2, NIV

I will bring the most wicked of the nations to take possession of their houses; I will put an end to the pride of the mighty, and their sanctuaries will be desecrated.
Ezekiel 7:24, NIV

Pride, therefore, should be removed from our character and from our lives. Ask the Holy Spirit to show you where you have pride in your heart. Everything we are and everything we have was given to us because God loves us and He is the one taking care of us. Our life could have been snuffed out at any time; but God is the one who allows breath to come into our lungs to remain alive. Be thankful for life and everything that is placed in our hands. We did not do this on our own, God was helping us.

Take some time to listen to what God is saying about this smooth stone of *Humility*. Do you really want this humility? Intimidation will have no voice in our life when you possess this smooth stone; *Humility*.

Let's pray a prayer of repentance to have all pride removed and take up the fifth smooth stone of *Humility*.

Take up the Smooth Stone of Humility

Father God, I ask You to help me to die to my attitudes and my character traits that are not of Your nature. Teach me the lessons I need to know in the difficulties that I face that I may learn to trust You with everything in my life. Give me wisdom and strength to endure and pass all of the trials and tests believing that You are with me and You love me no matter what I endure. Let it be Your glory and Your power working in me that helps me and sustains me.

I ask You to show me where I have been prideful. Show me where pride has been in my heart, in my thoughts, in my words, and in my actions. Father God, I ask that by Your Holy Spirit You would reach into my heart and remove pride from my heart, out of my thoughts, out of my words, and out of my actions. I do not want it there any longer.

I repent for allowing pride to enter into my heart. I will guard my heart against anything that would try to pollute it or damage my relationship with You. Forgive me for allowing pride to keep me away from You.

I now pick up this smooth stone of Humility and I choose to trust Your love for me and Your ability to take care of me. Thank you, God, for Your goodness towards me.

    The fifth smooth stone is *Humility*. To obtain this smooth stone one needs to allow the tests and trials in their life to cultivate *Humility* in their heart. Now we have added to our collection the fifth smooth stone.

Five Smooth Stones

These five smooth stones of truth will defeat the voice of intimidation that will try to rise up in our life. With these securely in our possession, we will not become paralyzed by the voice of intimidation and will be free to fulfill our purpose and destiny.

Take hold of this smooth stone of *Humility* and guard it in your heart as a priceless gem. This smooth stone is easily capable of slaying any voice of intimidation that would try to rise up against you. Though we are gathering these five smooth stones, *Identity, Authority, Love, Grace, and Humility, a Sling of Faith* will be required to set these five smooth stones into action.

We will begin to design our Sling of Faith so our smooth stones will become useful and active.

Questions

1. What is the definition of humility?

2. What is the way to humility?

3. What is the price we pay for humility?

4. What choices does a Christian have in the pursuit of humility?

5. Do the difficulties of tests and trials have any purpose in our lives?

6. What is it that needs to be removed from us so humility can have its rightful place?

7. How do we obtain humility?

Five Smooth Stones

8

The Sling of Faith

Now that we have our five smooth stones identified and collected, we need to mend and strengthen our sling of faith to propel these stones of *Identity, Authority, Love, Grace, and Humility* into action.

Let's begin by looking at Webster's definition of Faith. It is *confidence, belief, trust, to urge, to be convinced, to persuade, the unquestioning belief that does not require proof or evidence, complete trust, unquestioning belief in God.*[46]

So even if we can't see or touch what it is we are believing for, but if it is a promise in scripture or a word that God has spoken to us, then we should have unquestioning belief and confidence that we can have what God has said.

The Bible definition of faith is;

Now faith is being sure of what we hope for and certain of what we do not see.
Hebrew 11:1, NIV

Faith is believing a promise from God is true even when we do not see it. We are sure of what we hope for because it is a promise God has given us in scripture or has spoken to us personally. It is not a reality that we can see at the moment otherwise we wouldn't need faith to obtain it.

Five Smooth Stones

Faith is being sure of the promise we are hoping for will come to pass even though in the physical world we do not see it. The universe, stars, planets, and earth were all formed and set into place by God's word. They were made and crafted out of material that was not seen. That which is seen was not made out of what was visible, but that which was invisible. Faith is the substance of something unseen until it is seen.

When we hear God speak to us to do a specific action or to go a certain place, we do not always know all of the steps that it will take, but by faith we begin to take some steps. If we have faith in our ability to hear God, and we are obedient to do what He asks us to do, then something good will come from it. When believing in faith for something that we do not possess, when we hear God tell us to take an action step of faith toward that desire, we have a choice to either step out in faith and take a risk or to stand still. Faith is taking a risk.

The definition of risk is; *the potential of gaining or losing something of value such as physical health, social status, emotional well-being, or financial wealth. These can all be gained or lost when taking a risk. Risk can also be defined as the intentional interaction with uncertainty. It is an unpredictable and uncontrollable outcome.*[47]

Everyone takes a risk when they wake up each morning and considers their day. It is another level of risk to leave the house and go to school or to work each day. Then we experience greater risks when we start a new job or relocate to a different city. If we are sick, believing in God's promises for health, is

The Sling of Faith

taking a step of faith. Everyone has been given a measure of faith. We can increase our faith by reading the scriptures and having a relationship with God, Jesus, and the Holy Spirit. We want our faith to grow so it becomes strong faith and then great faith!

. . . but rather think of yourself with sober judgment in accordance with the measure of faith God has given you.
Romans 12:3b, NIV

Many Bible characters listed in Hebrews 11 had faith. All of these people were simply living out their lives, putting their trust in God, and at some point they took a huge step of risk. They walked across the dry bed of the Red Sea while God opened up the waters that looked like mountains on each side. This took faith that the waters would not come back down upon them drowning them and all their children. They conquered kingdoms, administered justice, sat next to lions whose mouths did not devour them, stepped into a fiery furnace and were not burned, rerouted armies and so much more all by faith. Yet, they died without seeing the promise they were believing for, Jesus.

Faith is made up of knowledge, belief, and trust.[48]

First comes knowledge. People who have not heard the good news of the gospel, or have not read their Bibles do not know what it says. How can someone believe when they have not heard anyone speak to them about what is written in the Bible?

If we do not have the knowledge that God can heal us and answer our prayer then we will remain sick and not know that

Five Smooth Stones

we can receive help. If we are ignorant of what is written in the Bible then we will not have knowledge of what belongs to us through the cross of Jesus Christ.

How, then, can they call on the one they have not believed in? And how can they believe in the one of whom they have not heard? And how can they hear without someone preaching to them?

Romans 10:14, NIV

We have to hear or read something to be informed of a fact before we can believe it. This comes from reading, studying, and speaking the truths about God and the Bible. Then comes faith.

Faith comes by hearing. We must hear the message so that we may know what the truth is so we can believe. Once we hear the truth of what belongs to us through our inheritance in Jesus Christ, then we can begin believing in those promises. Our faith will begin to grow as we believe and see answered prayer. God will be faithful to us and each day we will see His goodness causing faith to grow in our heart.

A measure of knowledge is essential to faith. We need to search the Scriptures and learn what they say concerning Christ and His salvation. We need to hear the truth and receive it in our hearts. The Holy Spirit will give us knowledge and understanding as we read and meditate on the word of truth. To know the good news, the forgiveness of sin, being adopted into the family of God, and countless other blessings will increase our faith.

As we hear wisdom and knowledge of scripture, we begin to

understand how they apply to us. We begin to rest in God's peace because we believe that He loves us and is taking care of us. As we accept this knowledge in our hearts, belief is being planted in the soil of our hearts. Our minds will be renewed, and we begin to have faith for God's promises to come into our life.

Second, we must believe with our hearts. Believing with our hearts that God is good and able to do what His word says. Believing with our hearts becomes as a guard to the things that come to take away our peace. Out of our heart flow all the issues of life. So, if we give our hearts good nutrition of encouragement, edification, exhortation and healthy thoughts of how God sees us, our hearts will be spiritually healthy and vibrant.

When our minds and hearts believe that Jesus is the truth, that He is God. He is our Savior, the Redeemer of all men, and the Father of His children, faith will grow inside of us. The mind and heart will come to believe the blood of Jesus Christ cleanses from all sin and sickness. We grow in our belief that Jesus' sacrifice was complete and fully accepted by God to wash away man's sin. Because of this truth, man can believe in Jesus and know without a doubt he is not condemned, but greatly loved. We can believe the word of God just as it would be a legal document or the testimony of our father or dear friend.

We accept man's testimony, but God's testimony is greater because it is the testimony of God, which he has given about his Son.

1 John 5:9, NIV

The third component of faith is trust. Trust is the lifeblood of faith. It is having full confidence that whatever God has said He will do. He will indeed do all He says. Trust is having complete confidence that God hears us when we ask Him for help, and He will give us that help. This trust is having complete confidence that God gave us a purpose, and He will help us to fulfill all He has promised us.

A deeper relationship with God will be established based on our trust in God as we talk with Him each day.

In a close relationship, trust develops. Each one is there for the other. They will not let each other down.

As we are submitted to walking according to His ways and obedient to do what He says in the word, we begin to hear His voice more clearly. Trust will be established in our relationship with Him.

Those who know your name will trust in you, for you Lord, have never forsaken those who seek you.
Psalm 9:10, NIV

We can trust God, having complete faith in Him because He loves us and is able to take care of us in every situation and circumstance that comes along. We only need to ask for help. We are encouraged to never let faith escape us. Faith should be bound around our necks and written upon our hearts.

God knows where He wants to take each of us and how to get us there. It will take a heart that trusts him, even when we don't fully understand the journey.

The Sling of Faith

Bind them upon our heart forever; fasten them around your neck.
Proverbs 6:21, NIV

Many pioneers before us began their journey not knowing exactly where their road would take them. However, they had faith to step out and keep going. If no one blazes a trail, there will never be a road to travel. With our trust in God, we will be trailblazers because that is who God is for us. All we have to do is follow Him.

When trust is established in our hearts, it will manifest in our lives. It will be evident in the way we talk and the way we walk. Our words and actions will agree, having the same focus. One who trusts becomes a doer of what is written in the Bible, and not just a hearer of it. When we are doers of the Word, faith is put into action.

Most people do not share Christ with others or step out to pray for them because they're afraid of being embarrassed or rejected because what they prayed for does not happen. However, if anyone wants to see God move upon the people around them, taking a risk is part of stepping out. Faith walked-out means risk-taking is a normal part of the believer's life. When people are sick or hurting, they almost always welcome someone to support them with prayer or show they care.

Do not merely listen to the word, and so deceive yourselves. Do what it says.
James 1:22, NIV

Five Smooth Stones

Faith begins with knowledge. Then faith believes with the heart and mind. This develops trust. Faith believes that Christ is what He said He is, and knows that He will do what He has promised to do. When we have faith, we have so much trust that we are willing to take a step of risk. Our faith becomes an action step.

Faith is a manifestation of the fruit of the Spirit. The fruit of faith will grow under the right conditions. Faith becomes strengthened when we exercise it by believing and hoping for a desire to come to pass. Muscles need to be exercised in order to grow, so does faith. Believing and standing in faith over a period of time for a promise God has given us will cause one to have a greater faith.

Being willing to go through a process to get a desired outcome strengthens our faith. Taking the steps God requires in order to move in a certain direction builds our faith and helps us to learn to hear God's voice and follow His leading.

Consequently, faith comes from hearing the message and the message is heard through the word of Christ.

Romans 10:17, NIV

Faith grows in a positive speaking environment. The words we speak should be in alignment with the hopes we have in our hearts. Negative words that are opposite of what God says will destroy faith. When we doubt God's promises as true, we cannot expect to receive anything from Him. Without faith, it is impossible to please God. Ask God to increase your faith.

The Sling of Faith

> *Immediately the boy's father exclaimed, "I do believe; help me overcome my unbelief!*
>
> Mark 9:24, NIV

We develop faith by stepping out just as David used his sling to propel a stone to kill an animal, and then to kill Goliath. This type of confidence propels us to move ahead with knowing, and believing, and trusting in God. We come to a place of confidence in God and in His Word that He will do for us what He says He will.

When the Israelites came out of Babylonian captivity, they came out with a conquering faith. They were a remnant people that had faith to overcome. Faith is a humbling position because it is putting our trust in God and not in our own abilities. Faith is the acceptance of a place of being completely dependent on God. One must be free from the glory of men, and of self, content to be nothing. Out of this nothingness, faith grows strong.[49]

We all have been given a measure of faith when we first believed in Jesus Christ our Savior. God knows that we live in a fallen and sinful world. Jesus had compassion for us because He understands what we face. He knows how we feel, and what we have to overcome. He understands all the tests and trials that come our way. He has given us the Holy Spirit to walk with us, to comfort us, and to help us. The Holy Spirit is a promise given to us, who speaks from the heart of a loving Father to his children.

> *. . . being confident of this, that he who began a good work in you will carry it on to completion until the day of Christ Jesus.*
>
> Philippians 1:6, NIV

Five Smooth Stones

We all want to live our lives knowing who we are and what our purpose is. It will take faith in what God says about us and faith in the plans He has for us to walk out those purposes.

In order to overcome intimidation, we will need a *Sling of Faith* to put our five smooth stones; *Identity, Authority, Love, Grace,* and *Humility* into action.

Let's ask God to increase and strengthen our *Faith*.

Take Hold of the Sling of Faith

Dear Heavenly Father, I thank You for the seed of Faith that You have given to me. I ask You to increase my faith as I read Your Word and take hold of Your promises. I ask You for understanding and revelation of Your Word so my faith can grow. I ask You to water this Faith in my heart so the roots will go down deep into my life.

When I have cares and worries I will bring them to You so this Faith inside of me does not become choked out by the difficult circumstances and situations. I allow You to test my heart so I can exercise my Faith. Help me to keep my heart soft and pliable so You can mold me into the vessel I am supposed to be. I ask You Father to increase and strengthen my Faith.

As I am obedient to what You are saying to me and I will take action steps to be a person of Great Faith. I love and trust You with my life. You said that Faith works by love, therefore my Faith is alive and well. Amen.

Our *Sling of Faith* is alive and well. As we practice using this *Sling of Faith*, we will be able to propel our five smooth stones to slay the spirit of intimidation that comes face to face with us. We will say like David,

This day the Lord will hand you over to me, and I'll strike you down and cut off your head. Today I will give the carcasses of the Philistine army to the birds of the air and the beasts of the earth and the whole world will know that there is a God in Israel.
1 Samuel 17:46, NIV

Five Smooth Stones

Questions

1. What is the Biblical definition of faith?

2. Does everyone have faith? How much faith?

3. What destroys faith?

4. What three components make up faith?

5. List some things that will cause your faith to grow.

Epilogue

David had only a sling and some stones in his bag to protect himself and his sheep from natural predators that would attempt to harm them. David loved God, he worshipped God, he trusted that God was with him, and would help him take care of the sheep in his pasture. We need God's help also, to take care of the pasture of our lives; our families, and of our territories. The phrase "do not fear" or "fear not" appears in the Bible 365 times.[50] One "fear not" for every day of the year.

David became skilled using the simple tools in his hands to guard himself and his flock from destruction. This young boy was alone in his pasture of sheep with only a sling, and some stones, and the God he worshipped and loved. This is how he stood against the predators that threatened their safety, every day of the year. David had everything he needed.

God has given us everything we need to overcome every obstacle in our life also. God did not leave us alone in our own pasture of life. As we learn how to use our sling of faith in the little things, we become more skilled to use our sling of faith in the bigger things. Each time David protected his sheep from predators, he practiced using the gifts and talents he was given to overcome obstacles.

The tests and trials in our lives can be used to our advantage, making us stronger and wiser. They were never

Five Smooth Stones

meant to defeat us. They are actually opportunities for us to grow and mature in our character. Pride is removed from us as we mature in sufferings. David drew upon his experience as a shepherd in the Judean desert when he wrote this Psalm.

The Lord is my shepherd, I shall not be in want. He makes me lie down in green pastures he leads me beside quiet waters he restores my soul. He guides me in paths of righteousness for his name's sake. Even though I walk through the valley of the shadow of death, I will fear no evil, for you are with me; your rod and your staff, they comfort me. You prepare a table before me in the presence of my enemies. You anoint my head with oil; my cup overflows. Surely goodness and love will follow me all the days of my life, and I will dwell in the house of the Lord forever.

Psalm 23, NIV

The contrast between darkness and light is intensified in the desert. Walking after sundown can be deadly. Dark, narrow ravines are ideal hiding places for predators. Shepherds have to lead their sheep through these narrow places to get to better grazing pastures.[51]

So, it is with us. When we are in a wilderness season and the way seems difficult and overwhelming, it is hard to find any pleasure, joy or happiness. It may feel like we are going through a narrow place because of the pressing-in of circumstances that weigh on us.

We can reach inside our bags of smooth stones, and pull out our stone of *Identity* to help us remember we are sons and daughters of the God Most High and He has promised to always be with us. Father God sees our situations and has not forgotten us. He tells us in Psalm 23 not to fear because He is with us. He promises us that goodness and love are our companions that follow us.

We can remember the truth about the *Authority* that has been given to us. We can command fear to leave us because it is a spirit and must obey us. We have all authority over evil spirits. In circumstances we must discern whether it is God's voice speaking or a strange voice speaking. If it is God's voice, we will be able to recognize His gentle voice and obey what He says. If it is another voice, we have been given authority to command it to leave, giving it no place in our territory.

At a point in my life, I realized the love I once had for the Lord escaped me. Focusing only on my problems allowed fear to come in that eroded at my Christ-given *Identity*. The freedom I once felt in God's grace became legalistic because I was no longer trusting in God's ability to help me work through difficulties. This all caused my authority in Christ to dissipate.

When we lose our intimate relationship with the Lord, we lose everything. Any valuable relationship will require time and attention. If we become too busy working at our jobs and trusting in our own abilities to make financial ends meet, we no longer are looking to God as our provider to meet our needs. Worry and anxiety begin to choke out the Word of God in us. Family relationships become stressed due to strife and unforgiveness. All of these things make us vulnerable to feeling fearful and intimidated.

The voice of intimidation yelled and taunted me for many

Five Smooth Stones

years saying, "Who do you think you are?" "You can't do that?" "You are not going to be able to pay your bills?" "Nobody loves you!" "You will always be alone!" "There is no hope for you!" "You have made too many mistakes to ever do anything worthwhile!" "God lied to you!" "God is not with you!" "You are doomed!" "No one will be there to help you!" "So where is your God now?"

When you know what God says about you and who you are, you can stand against the difficult winds that threaten your stability. I knew in the core of my identity that God loved me and He would help me, but because of the storms I felt battered and depleted within my emotions and my mind.

When I received this prophetic word in 2012, I understood how the difficulties and disappointments had erased the promises God had written on the chalkboard of my heart. Now, I had little strength and little hope of seeing these promises ever become a reality. I felt drained of all hope, feeling completely defeated.

When I meditated on this prophetic word, it stirred up life inside of me that I didn't know existed. I could feel a spark of hope ignite in the ashes of my soul that once had a flame of fire. The tentacles of grief that had taken root in my soul began to lose their hold on me. This word brought hope that I could live again. However, I had to search to find these five principles, these five truths, these five smooth stones so I could take hold of my life again in Christ.

I purchased books, CDs and teachings on identity, authority, love, grace, humility, and faith to rebuild and restore

Epilogue

the foundations that slipped out of my life. This enabled me to understand to some extent, how they slipped away and what I needed to do to rebuild them.

This enabled me to be who I was meant to be and do what I was created to do. By searching and examining these five smooth stones of *Identity, Authority, Love, Grace,* and *Humility,* I was able to collect them back into my possession. As I examined them, brushed off the pollutants of clay causing them to be smooth again, and placed them back into the knapsack of my heart, I embraced faith again.

David also carefully examined his five smooth stones in the water brook, placed them in his shepherd's bag and took hold of his sling.

Then he took his staff in his hand, chose five smooth stones from the stream, put them in the pouch of his shepherd's bag and, with his sling in his hand, approached the Philistine.
1 Samuel 17:40, NIV

The word *stones* in this scripture mean a "rock, having a specific balance, strength and stability, or a place of refuge" in Hebrew. *Rock* is a title of God, with a focus on strength and stability, a place of refuge.[52]

The Lord is my rock, my fortress and my deliverer; my God is my rock, in whom I take refuse. He is my shield and the horn of my salvation, my stronghold.
Psalm 18:2, NIV

Five Smooth Stones

This caused my heart to beat again with hope for my future.

When we possess our *Identity* in Christ, the *Authority* He has given us, the *Grace* He provides for us, the Love He offers us, and die to our self-nature while embracing *Humility*, we will easily recognize intimidation and have the courage to overcome any situation or circumstance that challenges us. We can have great *Faith* that keeps us stable, moving toward our goal!

Each of us has a book written by the hand of God in heaven that contains the plans and purposes for our lives. There is a life-course designed specifically for each person placed on earth to fulfill after they have become born again. As we all God to direct and lead us, we will be well able to fulfill those purposes.

God has given us everything we need to walk out a victorious Christian life. This walk will not be without the opposition of a Goliath speaking words of intimidation to oppose and challenge us. These forces do not originate with flesh and blood, but are spiritual forces.

For our struggle is not against flesh and blood but against the rulers, against the authorities, against the powers of this dark world and against the spiritual forces of evil in the heavenly realms.
                                                                Ephesians 6:12, NIV

These five stones must be made smooth and polished to

work well. Rocks are made smooth by the continuous flow of water over them. Our thoughts and the things we contemplate on will need the water of the Word of God to wash over them to cleanse and purify them.

The Word of God in scripture is referred to as water. We polish our five smooth stones with the water of the truth of the Word of God. This washes away all the lies that have been spoken to us or that we believed removing them from our hearts and minds.

These five smooth stones are truths God gives us in His inspired Word, the Bible. We can overcome the spirit of fear and intimidation that stands before us by applying God Word to our lives.

Your life is a gift with a purpose. As you activate your *Sling of Faith* and secure these five smooth stones, *Identity, Authority, Love, Grace*, and *Humility*, you will slay the voice of intimidation and fearlessly run the race set before you.

> *Therefore, since we are surrounded by such a great cloud of witnesses, let us throw off everything that hinders and the sin that so easily entangles, and let us run with perseverance the race marked out for us.*
> Hebrews 12:1, NIV

Your life-course is written in a book in Heaven, and is waiting for you to fulfill once you become a Christian by receiving Jesus Christ as your Savior.

Five Smooth Stones

God is the author and finisher of your life. He sent the Holy Spirit to help you, work with you, and comfort you along your journey. You are well equipped with your sling of faith and your five smooth stones to slay every voice of intimidation so you can fulfill your purpose!

Answers

Chapter One - Voice of the Lord

1. What are some examples of God speaking to people in the Bible?

Genesis 3:8a, "Then the man and his wife heard the sound of the Lord God as he was walking in the garden in the cool of the day."

Genesis 6:13-22, God spoke to Noah and told him to build an ark.

God spoke to Abram in Genesis 12:1-3, telling him to leave his country and go to a place that He would eventually show him.

Moses encountered the Lord in a fiery bush in Exodus 3, and heard God speak to him.

Exodus 19, Moses heard God's voice through thunder and lightning on Mount Sinai.

Revelation 1:15, John heard the voice of the Lord as the sound of many waters.

Elijah heard the voice of God on the mountain at Horeb in 1 Kings 19:11.

Samuel heard the voice of God in 1 Samuel 3. While Samuel lie asleep, the Lord called out to him.

Five Smooth Stones

David heard the Spirit of God moving in the tops of the mulberry trees in II Samuel 5:24-25. God told David when he heard the sound in the mulberry trees, he was to move quickly to attack the Philistine army, because God was going before him in the battle.

David got a strategy from God and had victory over his enemy. Isaiah heard God's voice in Isaiah 6:8a, "Then I heard the voice of the Lord saying, 'Whom shall I send? And who will go for us?'"

The voice of the Lord will witness of Christ's divinity. Matthew 17:5, "While he was still speaking, a bright cloud enveloped them, and a voice from the cloud said, 'This is my Son, whom I love; with him I am well pleased. Listen to him!'"

2. What are some purposes for God to speak?

Has creative power
Brings order out of chaos
His words move and hover over us
For relationship and fellowship
For direction in your life
For instructions to overcome obstacles
To speak life into people
Calls people out from an ordinary life
Sends people to certain places for certain purposes
Brings peace and draws us out of hiding
Gives encouragement
Provide for us and protect us.
His words comfort, edify and encourage.
God gives directions, instructions, and warnings.
When making decisions God gives instructions to navigate.

Answers

The voice of the Lord will witness of Christ's divinity.
God proceeded to instruct Samuel about the future.
To show us the Father's love towards us

3. How many times in scriptures does God say, "Thus says the Lord."

More than one thousand times God spoke, "Thus says the Lord."

4. What does God's voice sound like?

It is a force or wind that moves upon us, earth, and heaven.
Adam heard the sound of God's presence stirring in the wind.
God was very personal and detailed in giving instructions.
Abraham heard God clearly to leave his country to a place he didn't know.

Abraham was only given the general direction to go.
Moses encountered the Lord in a firey bush hearing God speak.
Moses heard God's voice in the thunder and lightning.
John heard God's voice as the sound of many rushing waters
Elijah heard God's voice on a mountain as a gentle quiet whisper
While Samuel lay sleeping on his bed the Lord called out to him 3 times.

David heard God moving in the tops of the mulberry trees
Peter, James, and John heard God's voice speak from a cloud.
Ezekiel described God's voice as 'the roar of rushing waters.'
The Book of Revelation depicts the heavenly realm as a noisy place where tons of information was constantly being processed and conveyed to earth.

Five Smooth Stones

5. What are some ways the world speaks to us?

Loud cultural norms
Peer pressures
Media and technology
Accepted societal expectations.
Busy going to jobs
How to care for families
Attending social events with their influences.
Attending school functions
Hobbies of various kinds

6. What happens to people when they hear God's voice?

Causes them to live.
Caused them to fall on their face, become afraid with reverence.
Brought a humble realization of the holiness of God.
Brought attention to what God was telling them
Caused Peter to stop talking, listen, and take a humble position.
Elijah responded by getting up and leave his place of hiding in a cave.
Samuel acknowledged God's voice and responded.
Isaiah felt unworthy because he could see the holiness of God

Answers

Chapter Two – The Voice of Intimidation

1. What is the meaning of Canaanite?

Canaanite means to humiliate, and intimidate.
This is an "ite" that humiliates and intimidates a person.
Humiliation robs from us by causing us to feel weak.
The enemy will abuse, victimize, and shame people to make them feel like they do not deserve to be loved or blessed.

2. What are the consequences if we do not remove intimidation from our lives?

This is what will be lost in our lives if we do not drive fear out of our life. Numbers 33:55, 56, "But if you do not drive out the inhabitants of the land, those you allow to remain will become barbs in your eyes and thorns in your sides. They will give you trouble in the land where you live. And then I will do to you what I plan to do to them."

3. What will we gain if we do remove intimidation from our lives?

This is what we gain when we drive out the "ites" from our land.
We will be blessed more than any other people.
Deuteronomy 7:13, "And He will love you and bless you and increase your numbers. He will bless the fruit of your womb, the crops of your land--your grain, new wine and oil--the calves of your herds and the lambs of your flocks in the land that he swore to your forefathers to give you."

Five Smooth Stones

4. What three parts of our personhood do we sense and identify fear?

When fear comes, we sense and identify it in three parts of our being.
Soul; we can recognize fear in our soul, our mind, will, and emotions.
We can recognize fear with our mind, because of the thoughts it causes us to have. We recognize fear with our emotions by the feelings it produces in us. We recognize fear with our will, because it causes us to respond in a certain way, either to flee from it, or take a stand against it.

Physical body; we can discern fear with our physical body, because our body may become stiff or in a paralyzed state when it is exposed to fear. When we are fearful we may have a bodily response of our heart rate increasing. Our faces may take on a different countenance that looks worried or has a shocked looked. Our eyes may become enlarged and fixed in response to fear.

Spirit; we can recognize fear with our spirit. It will witness deep inside of us. A believer's intuition should be able to discern rightly when fear is present and even where it is coming from.

5. What are some guidelines God gives us for living?

God gave us a new commandment in Matthew 22:37-39 by telling us to love the Lord our God with all our heart, with all our soul, with all our mind, and then to also love our neighbors as ourselves.

6. What two ways do we quiet the sensory overload the world's

environment sends to our body, soul, and spirit?

One way is avoidance of sensory overload. The process of avoidance involves creating a more quiet and orderly environment in which to live. This includes keeping noise and sensory input to a minimum, reducing the sense of clutter. To prevent sensory overload, it is important to rest before big events and focus attention and energy on one thing at a time.

Second way is to set limits on sensory overload.
Setting limits involves restricting the amount of time spent on various activities and selecting settings to carefully avoid crowds and noise.

6. What are some disorders associated with sensory overload?

Sensory overload has been found to be associated with disorders such as fibromyalgia, chronic fatigue syndrome, posttraumatic stress disorder, autistic spectrum disorders, generalized anxiety disorder, schizophrenia, synesthesia, and sensory processing disorder.

7. What causes our souls to become weary and easily subject to whatever is in the environment?

An overload of stimulation causes the soul to become weary. Things that do this are: a constant intake of cell phones, messages, computer games, televisions, DVD movies, and noise. Listening to and viewing many violent things that threaten our well-being causes a wearing down of our soul.
Much of what we view through technology is traumatic and threatening to our well-being because of the violent nature.

Five Smooth Stones

Our environment becomes less peaceful as we allow this to rob us of peace. It causes an imbalance to our well-being.

Answers

Chapter Three – First Smooth Stone – Identity

1. What is identity?

Identity is the condition or fact of being the same or exactly alike, sameness; oneness. (God created us to have the same likeness that He has.)
Identity is also, the condition or fact of being a specific person or thing with individuality. (Even though we have the same likeness as God our Creator, each person is unique just as every snowflake has its own characteristics.)
The characteristics and qualities of a person considered collectively and regarded as essential to that person's self-awareness.
The condition of being the same as a person or thing described or claimed.

2. What does it mean that we have the same likeness of God?

God created us to have the same likeness as He has.
Genesis 1:27 says, "So God created man in his own image, in the image of God created he him, male and female created he them."
Male and female are both made in the likeness of God.
We have the same identity that God has.
We were made in His image.
His image has three parts; a spirit, a soul, and a body.

3. Describe the three parts that make up the human being.

The Bible explains that we are triune beings.
We are a spirit, with a soul, which is our mind, our will, and our emotions, and we live in a physical body.
God made us this way so we could live and function on the earth.

Five Smooth Stones

First, we are a spirit being, just as God is a spirit.
John 4:24a, "God is Spirit."
Second, we have a soul consisting of a mind to think with.
In our soul, is our will to make decisions with and choices for ourselves.
Also in our soul, we have emotions that cause us to have feelings about our surroundings and for one another.
Third, God gave us a physical body to inhabit while we are here on earth. This is how we look and it provides a means to function in the earth.
God told us to be fruitful and multiply and to love God and one another.

4. After God who is the most influential that imparts identity to us?

The next influential source of our identity comes from our parents.
God blessed marriage between a man and a woman and purposed for them to be fruitful and multiply the earth by having children.
The home was to have a father and a mother who were meant to be loving parents who provide a safe and secure environment for their family.
Their family was to be an example of what family looks like in heaven.
Our parents were meant to reinforce our identity by loving us and properly training us to love God and our neighbors.
God sets a father and mother in the home as the protector, provider, and comforter for the children.
God is also our Father in heaven who is our protector, provider, and comforter.
The father in the home provides the family members with a warm

and safe home to live in, with enough food to eat, and clothes to wear.

The father helps the children to fulfill their dreams by helping them through college or on a career path that is fulfilling for them.

Fathers are given this position by God, as the head of the home. They are meant to provide safety and security for the family.

The father was meant to give their children a Godly identity to help them fulfill their calling and destiny.

The position of a father and mother was meant to be a blessing to their family.

God's identity was meant to be transferred from the father into the lives of the children, to give them a knowing of who they were created to be.

5. What things might hinder our identity being imparted into us?

If the father abuses his position over the family causing them to feel threatened, it destroys the strong identity the child was supposed to have imparted to them by their father.

When children grow up in abusive homes, they may not have a true identity of themselves.

This may cause them to be easily intimidated and fearful.

They may have negative emotions in their character and in their personality if their identity is not imparted to them the way God intended it to be while growing up in the home.

For those who grow up in a home where there is alcoholism, there is a strong sense of insecurity.

There may be little or no emotional stability and this allows much insecurity and fear of the future, fear of safety, and fear of what is going to happen next, and fear of anything that threatens their well-being.

Five Smooth Stones

Abuse and lies rob us of the identity we are meant to carry.

Everyone will need to receive their full identity from Father God through receiving Jesus Christ as their Savior.

This is how a person receives the identity they were meant to have.

We were all created by God having come from the first man and woman, Adam and Eve.

Because sin entered the world, we became separated from God and our identity became perverted.

In the Old Testament, the blood of lamb sacrifices were given to cleanse the people of sin.

When Jesus came into the world and died on the cross, he paid man's debt for sin in-full.

There is a requirement of man though, and that is to believe and accept the price Jesus paid for him.

Answers

Chapter Four – Second Smooth Stone – Authority

1. What does authority mean?

It is the power or right to give commands, enforce obedience, take action, or make final decisions, the position of one having such power.

Such power as delegated to another, authorization, warrant.
The power or influence resulting from knowledge, prestige.
The citation of a writing, decision, etc. in support of an opinion, an action.

It is delegated power or influence from knowledge, or a position, or an assignment.

2. What are some examples of people or positions that have authority?

Some examples of people or positions of authority are; parents, fathers and mothers, school teachers, church leaders, policemen, military officers, leaders in organizations, leaders in a business, employers, and of course God.

3. What is the purpose that these people or positions are given this authority?

To restrain evil
To protect innocent people
To provide a safe environment
To govern our own selves
To govern our family
To govern our territory, nation, country.

Five Smooth Stones

4. What kind of fruit do we see in families when authority is not imparted to the children?

Children raised in a home where parents are abusive will feel powerless to govern themselves because a righteous authority is not imparted into them.
Instead, the power to govern ourselves rightly will be removed from us.

When a child feels powerless, he will be unable to defend himself or to accomplish great things because he was made to feel that he didn't have the ability to accomplish great things.
The authoritative power God meant for us to have in our lives will instead be replaced by negative emotions such as fear, anger, rage, jealousy, envy, wrath, manipulation, control, hatred, and even murder.

The abuse of the father's power over his children, makes the child feel powerless or helpless, and it distorts their ability to govern their lives well.
Abuse of authority causes extreme damage to the family.

5. How much authority did Jesus have? How much authority do we have?

Jesus had all authority, given to him by the Father.
Believers of Jesus Christ have all authority, given to them by Jesus.

6. What are some things that take authority away from us?

Answers

Some things that take authority away from us are; when those in authority over us misuse their God-given delegated oversight over us.

This removes the power we were meant to have from God that gives us the ability to govern ourselves.

7. Why do these things remove authority from us?

These things remove authority from us because it causes us to feel powerless. When those who have authority over us misuse that right, the authority we are to receive does not get imparted to us and we are not empowered within ourselves to make righteous good decisions.

8. What is the result when the righteous use their authority?

When the righteous use their authority the people rejoice.

9. What is the result when the righteous do not use their authority?

When the righteous do not use their authority, the people mourn and perish.

10. In what ways can we receive authority in our lives?

We receive authority in our lives when we give our heart and lives to Jesus Christ. It is by having relationship, familiarity, and intimacy with God as our Father and Lord that we are given authority to govern ourselves, our families, and our land.

11. What is the power behind this authority in our lives?

Five Smooth Stones

The power behind our authority is God. God gave Adam and Eve dominion, but when they sinned and rebelled against God, they forfeited their dominion rights to satan. When Jesus Christ died for us and went to hell, He took these keys of authority away from satan and gave them back to man. Now man is given the authority to bind and loose on earth what God's will is in heaven. When Jesus left earth, he told his followers to wait in the upper room or a place where they could gather to pray and worship until the Holy Spirit came and endued them with power. The Holy Spirit did come, baptizing them with power to cast out devils, heal the sick and work miracles among the people.

12. What types of things does the Christians have authority over?

Christians have authority over all the works of the enemy; sin, sickness, demons, poverty, addictions, and every kind of disease.

13. What do we receive when we are baptism in the Holy Spirit?

The baptism of the Holy Spirit gives us power to be a witness of who God is. There are gifts and manifestations that are available to us with the baptism of the Holy Spirit.
In this baptism we receive a prayer language called 'tongues' that enables our spirit to communicate with God, and He to us.

Answers

Chapter Five - Third Smooth Stone – Love

1. What is a simple definition of love?

The definition of love is a deep and tender feeling of affection for or attachment or devotion to a person or persons.
It is an expression of one's love or affection.
It is a feeling of brotherhood and good will toward other people.
It is a strong liking for or interest in something.
It is a strong, usually passionate, affection of one person for another, based in part on sexual attraction.

2. What is the Bible definition of love and what does it look like?

The Bible definition of love is patience and kindness.
This love is not jealous and does not boast.
It is not proud and does not dishonor others.
This love does not seek things for themselves.
It does not become angry or have evil intents toward another.
This love does not rejoice over unrighteousness, but rejoices in truth.
Love endures all things and believes all things according to the will and ways of God.
This love hopes all things and is steadfast in all things.

3. What is the type of love that God has for us and what does that look like?

The type of love that God has for us is an Agape love.
It is supernatural and was demonstrated by Jesus dying on the cross and going to hell for us so we had an opportunity to be reconciled back to God the Father once again if that is what our free-will chooses.

Five Smooth Stones

4. What are some attributes of love in a marriage?

Some attributes of love in a marriage are: they choose one another.
They take full responsibility for that choice.
They protect one another.
They serve each other.
They are faithful towards one another.
They are able to be authentic with each other and can be who they say they are on a consistent basis.
They know how to be themselves and are safe to be with.
They allow others to know them by being transparent.
They honor and protect each other in their relationship.
The demonstrate self-control and do not manipulate to control others.
They communicate consistently in ways that people can hear and understand and receive.

5. How do we get this love inside of us?

Love is a seed planted in our hearts when we receive Jesus Christ as our Savior. It is a seed planted in us from the Spirit of God. It is a decision we make to receive Jesus Christ as our savior or not and it is up to us if we allow this seed to grow or not by reading the bible and having a relationship with the Lord on a daily basis.

6. How do we allow this love inside of us to grow according to this chapter?

This love seed is allowed to grow in us as we forgive others. To cultivate this kind of love in our hearts, we are required to forgive.

Love is like a fruit, it can grow or it can become stale and then rotten.

Each time we forgive, our fruit of love grows a little bigger, a little healthier and a little brighter.

When we do not forgive, this fruit begins to dry up within us and eventually becomes rotten and will, of course, smell bad.

Five Smooth Stones

Chapter Six - Fourth Smooth Stone – Grace

1. What is a simple definition of grace?

A simple definition of grace is God's unearned favor.
It is the unmerited favor of God toward human beings.
It is divine influence acting in a person to make the person pure, and morally strong. A special virtue, gift, or help given to a person by God.

2. Why was it hard for the Israelites to receive God's grace?

They were afraid to come into relationship with God because they didn't understand the grace God was offering to them.
They had come from Egypt where they lived by the law and did not know how to have a relationship with God by grace.
This happens often in the lives of many believers.
It is easier to have a list of what to do, and what not to do, however, grace is dependent upon relationship.
Grace is dependent upon hearing the voice of God.
Grace enables us, but the law requires us.

3. Why is having compassion greater than sacrifice?

God wants our hearts to be touched with compassion so we can affect the people around us.
It takes grace to fast, but it takes a greater grace to have a heart of compassion.
This compassion is a grace on us that will reset the moral compass in people's lives.
Grace allows people to move with compassion above sacrifice.

Answers

4. Why was Hezekiah miserable in the last 15 years of his life?

Hezekiah was miserable the last 15 years of his life because he refused to be thankful and recognize that what he had in wealth and respectful relationships, prestige position, to be healed of a deathly sickness and live another 15 years and prosper all those years was all because of God's kindness towards him.
The refusal for Hezekiah to be thankful and recognize that what he had was because of God's kindness towards him, was not God's will.

5. What is the difference in relationships between God promoting man and the world promoting man?

The difference in relationships between God promoting man and the world promoting man is when God promotes man, the man is brought closer into relationship with people and when the world promotes man, the man is removed from close relationship with the people.

6. Does man have any responsibility towards God when he by grace overcomes difficulties?

Man does have a responsibility towards God when grace allows him to overcome difficulties.
There should be some type of an acknowledgment we give to God in the form of thanks and sacrificial offering.
When God's favor is upon us there should be some form of acknowledgement on our part that blesses other people.
God's grace upon our lives was not meant for us to keep to ourselves, but to share with others.

Five Smooth Stones

7. How do we maintain grace in our lives?

We maintain grace in our lives by living by the spirit and not according to the things of the flesh.

8. What are some of the fruits of the flesh?

Some of the fruits of the flesh are sexual immorality, impurity, and debauchery; idolatry and witchcraft; hatred, discord, jealousy, fits of rage, selfish ambition, dissensions, factions, and envy; drunkenness, orgies, and the like.

9. What are some of the fruits of the spirit?

Some of the fruits of the spirit are love, joy, peace, patience, kindness, goodness, faithfulness, gentleness, and self-control.

Answers

Chapter Seven - Fifth Smooth Stone – Humility

1. What is the definition of humility?

The definition of humility is absence of vanity, showing respect, an unassuming attitude, low in rank without pretentions or attempting to impress others.

2. What is the way to humility?

The way to humility is by dying to self and our own selfish desires.

3. What is the price we pay for humility?

The price we pay for humility is the same price Jesus Christ paid. Jesus bought it for us through His own death, burial, and resurrection. We purchase it by dying to our own desires and wants. We pay the price when we do not get offended when someone talks bad about us or hurt us. We pay the price when we choose to bless them with our words and even with our finances instead of gossiping, complaining, belittle them, or having evil thoughts towards them. We pay the price of humility by walking in forgiveness, gentleness, kindness, longsuffering, and loving in the midst of jealousy and hatred. We pay for humility by keeping our heart in a peaceful state even in the midst of the chaos around us. By praying for those who misuse us and then treating them with the same kindness God treats us with.

Five Smooth Stones

4. What choices does the Christian have in the pursuit of humility?

Every Christian is presented with a choice to pursue humility.
In the pursuit of humility, we have a choice to either face fear or flee from the fear.
If we face the difficulty and walk through it correctly then we will learn humility.
If we flee difficulty, we prevent being delivered from all that can humble us.
If a person does flee from a difficulty, then he will go around the same mountain again until he comes to a similar situation and learns the lesson of being humble.

5. Do the difficulties of tests and trials have any purpose in our lives?

Tests and trails are not from God, but God will use them so we learn to become dependent on Him.
The people of Israel were learning to depend on God as their Father for their needs instead of themselves, or the government of Egypt.
This was a test that lasted forty years to bring thm to a place of humility and dependent on God.

6. What needs to be removed from us so humility can have its rightful place?

Pride. This is what will need to be remove from us so humility can take its rightful place. We will either humble ourselves or God will do it for us.
The latter is much more painful than the first.
Even nations that are overly prideful God says He will bring an

Answers

end to.

7. How do we obtain humility?

We obtain humility by allowing the tests and trials in our lives to cultivate humility in our hearts and in our character.

Five Smooth Stones

Chapter Eight - The Sling of Faith

1. What is the biblical definition of faith?

The Biblical definition of faith is being sure of what we hope for and certain of what we do not see will be seen. When we have a promise from God we believe it to be true even when we do not have it but having confidence that we will obtain it.

2. Does everyone have faith? How much faith?

Everyone has faith. All have been given a measure of faith?

3. What destroys *faith?*

Negativity destroys faith.

4. What three components are faith made of up?

Faith is comprised of knowledge, belief, and trust.

5. What are some things that will cause your faith to grow?

Things that will cause faith to grow are reading and studying scripture.
Believing the promises of God cause faith to grow.
Exercising the Word of Truth by putting it to use and acting on it cause faith to grow.
Our trials and tests will cause us to seek help from God.
When we think on positive things instead of negative things our faith will grow.
We can ask God to increase our faith.

Endnotes

Chapter One – The Voice of the Lord

1. The Strongest Strong's Exhaustive Concordance of the Bible, by James Strong, LL.D. ST.D. Copyright 2001 by Zondervan, Grand Rapids, Michigan 49530 ISBN 978-0-310- 23343-5
2. Spirit Talk Hearing the Voice of God Copyright 2005 by Larry Randolph MorningStar Publications A Division of MorningStar Fellowship Church 375 Star Light Drive Fort Mill SC 29715 International Standard Book Number 1-929371-51-9; 978-1-929371- 51-8

Chapter Two – The Voice of Intimidation

3. Webster's New World College Dictionary Fifth Edition The Official Dictionary of The Associated Press Stylebook ISBN: 978-0- 544-16553-3
4. Ibid
5. Voice of the Apostles 2013, Global Awakening 1451 Clark Street Mechanicsburg, PA 17055, Mark Chironna
6. Ibid
7. Ibid
8. Ibid
9. https://en.wikipedia.org/wiki/Sensory_overload
10. Ibid
11. Ibid
12. http://medical-dictionary.thefreedictionary.com/
13. Ibid
14. *Voice of the Apostles 2013, Global Awakening* 1451 Clark Street Mechanicsburg, PA 17055, Mark Chironna
15. Ibid
16. www.dictionary.com/browse/weariness
17. Overcoming the Goliath of Fear CD Publish and Copyright Shekinah 2013 Barbara J. Yoder
18. Ibid

Five Smooth Stones

Chapter Three – First Smooth Stone – Identity

19. Webster's New World College Dictionary Fifth Edition The Official Dictionary of The Associated Press Stylebook ISBN: 978-0- 544-16553-32
20. Who Am I & Why Am I Here Copyright 2005 Dr. Bill Hamon Destiny Image Publishers Inc. PO Box 310 Shippensburg, PA 17257-0310 ISBN 0-7684-2255-8
21. Ibid
22. Recipe for a Fear-Free- Free Life, DVD 2013 Dawna De Silva, Bethel Media 5090 Caterpillar Road Redding, CA 96003
23. Ibid
24. Ibid
25. Higher Living Leadership; Influence Societal Design as an Instrument of Justice copyright 2017 Dr. Melodye Hilton Outskirts Press, Inc. http://222.outskirtspress.com ISBN: 978-1-5787-8237-7
26. Ibid
27. Addictions by Henry W. Wright Pleasant Valley Church, Inc. 4178 Crest Highway Thomaston, Georgia 30286 copyright 2003 Pleasant Valley Publications
28. Ibid

Chapter Four – Second Smooth Stone -- Authority

29. Webster's New World College Dictionary Fifth Edition The Official Dictionary of The Associated Press Stylebook ISBN: 978-0- 544-16553-3
30. Believer's Authority by Kenneth E. Hagin ISBN-23: 978-0- 89276-406-8 ISBN-10: 0-89276-406-6 (Formerly ISBN-10: 0- 89276-006-0) Copyright 1967, 1986 Rhema Bible Church AKA Kenneth Hagin Ministries, Inc.
31. The Strongest Strong's Exhaustive Concordance of the Bible, by James Strong, LL.D. ST.D. Copyright 2001 by Zondervan, Grand Rapids, Michigan 49530 ISBN 978-0-310-23343-5

Chapter Five – Third Smooth Stone -- Love

32. Webster's New World College Dictionary Fifth Edition The Official

Dictionary of The Associated Press Stylebook ISBN: 978-0- 544-16553-3

33. http://blogs.christianpost.com/better-than-i-deserve/different-types-of-love-found-in-the-bible-21799/

34. http://www.pewsocialtrends.org/2015/12/17/1-the-american-family-today/

35. http://www.universeofsymbolism.com/animals-that-mate-for-life.html

36. Keep Your Love On by Danny Silk Copyright 2013 ISBN 13: 978- 0-9884992-3-2

37. Ibid

Chapter Six – Fourth Smooth Stone -- Grace

38. Webster's New World College Dictionary Fifth Edition The Official Dictionary of The Associated Press Stylebook ISBN: 978-0- 544-16553-3

39. The Nature of Grace by Bill Johnson DVD

40. Ibid

41. Ibid

42. Spirit Talk Hearing the Voice of God, Copyright 2005 by Larry Randolph Morning- Star Publications A Division of MorningStar Fellowship Church 375 Star Light Drive Fort Mill SC 29715 International Standard Book Number 1-929371-51-9; 978-1-929371- 51-8

Chapter Seven - Fifth Smooth Stone -- Humility

43. Webster's New World College Dictionary Fifth Edition The Official Dictionary of The Associated Press Stylebook ISBN: 978-0- 544-16553-3

44. Humility, The Beauty of Holiness, by Andrew Murray, An Ichtus Publications edition, copyright 2014, ISB 10: 1502559560, ISBN 13: 978-1502550562

45. Ibid

Five Smooth Stones

Chapter Eight – The Sling of Faith

46. Webster's New World College Dictionary Fifth Edition The Official Dictionary of The Associated Press Stylebook ISBN: 978-0- 544-16553-3

47. https://en.wikipedia.org/wiki/Risk

48. All of Grace Copyright 2008 by Charles H Spurgeon BiblioBazaar

49. Ibid

Epilogue

50. http://www.answers.com/Q/How_many_times_is_the_word_fear_in_the_Bible

51. http://www.topbibleverses.com/how-do-i-live-without- fear Copyright 2006 Carey Kinsolving

52. The Strongest Strong's Exhaustive Concordance of the Bible, by James Strong, LL.D. ST.D. Copyright 2001 by Zondervan, Grand Rapids, Michigan 49530 ISBN 978-0-310- 23343-5

Bibliography

Books

All Scripture is taken from Thompson Chain-Reference Bible New International Version Copyright 1990 by The B.B. Kirkbride Bible Company, Inc. Indianapolis, Indiana

Webster's New World College Dictionary Fifth Edition The Official Dictionary of The Associated Press Stylebook ISBN: 978-0-544-16553-3

The Strongest Strong's Exhaustive Concordance of the Bible, by James Strong, LL.D. ST.D. Copyright 2001 by Zondervan, Grand Rapids, Michigan 49530 ISBN 978-0-310- 23343-5

Spirit Talk Hearing the Voice of God, Copyright 2005 by Larry Randolph MorningStar Publications A Division of MorningStar Fellowship Church 375 Star Light Drive Fort Mill SC 29715 International Standard Book Number 1-929371- 51-9; 978-1-929371-51-8

Believer's Authority, by Kenneth E. Hagin ISBN-23:978-0-89276-406-8 ISBN-10: 0-89276-406-6 Copyright 1967, 1986 Rhema Bible Church AKA Kenneth Hagin Ministries, Inc.

All of Grace, Copyright 2008 by Charles H Spurgeon BiblioBazaar

Humility, The Beauty of Holiness, Copyright 2014 by Andrew Murray, An Ichtus Publications edition ISB 10: 1502559560, ISBN 13: 978-1502550562

Who Am I & Why Am I Here, Copyright 2005 Dr. Bill Hamon Destiny Image Publishers Inc. PO Box 310 Shippensburg, PA 17257-0310 ISBN 0-7684-2255-8

Five Smooth Stones

Keep Your Love On, Copyright 2013 by Danny Silk Red Arrow Media, Redding, CA ISBN 13: 978-0-9884992-3-2

Addictions by Henry W. Wright Pleasant Valley Church, Inc. 4178 Crest Highway Thomaston, Georgia 30286 copyright 2003 Pleasant Valley Publications

Higher Living Leadership; Influence Societal Design as an Instrument of Justice copyright 2017 Dr. Melodye Hilton Outskirts Press, Inc. http://222.outskirtspress.com ISBN: 978-1-5787-8237-7

Conference
Voice of the Apostles 2013, Global Awakening 1451 Clark Street Mechanicsburg, PA 17055, Mark Chironna

CD's
Overcoming the Goliath of Fear CD Publish & Copyright Shekinah 2013 Barbara J. Yoder

DVD's
Recipe for a Fear-Free-Life, DVD 2013 Dawna De Silva, Bethel Media 50090 Caterpillar Road Redding, CA 96003
The Nature of Grace, DVD by Bill Johnson

Websites
http://blogs.christianpost.com/better-than-i- deserve/different-types-of-love-found-in-the-bible-21799/ (May 21, 2016)
https://en.wikipedia.org/wiki/Sensory_overload
www.dictionary.com/browse/weariess
http://www.pewsocialtrends.org/2015/12/17/1-the- american-family-today/
http://www.universeofsymbolism.com/animals-that- mate-for-life.html
http://www.answers.com/Q/How_many_times_is_the_ word_fear_in_the_Bible

Bibliography

http://medical-dictionary.thefreedictionary.com/
https://en.wikipedia.org/wiki/Risk
http://www.topbibleverses.com/how-do-i-live-without- fear
Copyright 2006 Carey Kinsolving

Five Smooth Stones

More from the Author

A Baptism of Fiery Love is Coming

The Holy Spirit is at work in every person's life wooing and pursuing them to return to a loving relationship with Father God their Creator. This an individual process walked out by each person.

The Holy Spirit wants to introduce himself to each one of us. He came to heal our hearts and our bodies that we may have an abundant life and share in His glory. This is the beginning of an era of seeing and experiencing God's glory.

Revealing God's Truth on Abortion

A Study Guide for *God, What is My Baby's Name?*

"Whether you are a woman who has suffered in silence over a past abortion, a family member or friend with a loved one who has had an abortion, or a pastor or counselor, this book will provide insight, strategy and a practical process to help restore hope and wholeness to broken lives."

Jane Hamon

God, What is My Baby's Name?

Jesus came to heal the brokenhearted. The brokenhearted are those who have suffered pain in their hearts. The brokenhearted are those who are grieving over a loss in their lives and have little hope. Because of the shame and guilt a woman and man experience when there is an abortion, they grieve in silence. There is nowhere to go to have this pain removed. The medical field can perform all kinds of marvelous things for our bodies, but there is only one that can heal the pain of a broken heart.

Five Smooth Stones

What Kind of Love is This?

Susan gave her life to Jesus during a Billy Graham television program. Later while working in a nursing home, she gained a burden to pray for the sick. She witnessed legs grow out, addictions leave, hips calcify causing patients to come off long-term bedrest, and a dementia patient begin to have a clear mind again. The pursuit of praying for the sick became her life ambition. Build your faith and un-lock miracles on this incredible journey of the supernatural.

Stop Steven, Stop

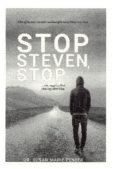

The trauma of losing a son to a chemical overdose hurled Susan into a grief that caused a brokenness of heart that was not able to find relief. Wholeness seemed impossible to obtain. While seeking her own healing, Susan not only obtained the healing of her broken-hearted condition but also leads the way for others who are brokenhearted to be made whole.

Healing the Broken-Hearted . . . Repairing Our Walls and Gates

Just as Nehemiah repaired the walls of Jerusalem, the broken-hearted need to repair walls to bring healing to their wounds. When our hearts become wounded with painful emotions, we hurt, which affects our decision-making and every area of lives. We may not even be aware of what has caused us to feel a pain inside. This is why God sent His Son Jesus Christ to earth to die for us; to bring healing to the broken-hearted.

More from the Author

For Speaking Engagements or Questions
Contact Susan Marie Pender
Susanmariepender@gmail.com
www.lilyofthevalleyhealing.com

Made in the USA
Middletown, DE
10 November 2022

14570712R00128